build better
z⌀diac
relationships

build better
z*o*diac
relationships

ALAN BUTLER

quantum
LONDON • NEW YORK • TORONTO • SYDNEY

quantum

An imprint of W. Foulsham & Co. Ltd
The Publishing House, Bennetts Close,
Cippenham, Slough, Berkshire, SL1 5AP, England

ISBN 0–572–02760-5

Printed in Great Britain by St Edmundsbury Press, Bury St Edmunds, Suffolk

Contents

Introduction

 elcome to *Build Better Zodiac Relationships*, the book that can tell you so much about your interactions with the world. How do you get on with Scorpios? Could you work comfortably with a Leo? Are you ever likely to find yourself in a romantic clinch with a Piscean? These and many other questions can be answered in the pages that follow.

So much of relationships at any level, when seen from an astrological perspective, depends on the way you, as an astrological sign type, relate to the world at large. Some zodiac sign types automatically mesh, whilst others clash. This book will tell you why some of your friendships work as well as they do – and why some don't – and can also offer a little advice on how to approach people you haven't been successful with in the past.

The first section of the book shows you how to compare your own zodiac sign with that of any other person. Let us imagine, for example, that you are born under the sign of Gemini. All you have to do is to go to the Gemini section and there you will find a comparison between your own zodiac sign and all the others. But since the 'day' on which an individual is born only represents part of the average person's nature, this book goes further.

In creating an individual, the Rising Sign is of particular importance. This is the zodiac sign that was coming over the eastern horizon at the time any person was born. On pages 130–41, you will find a series of easy-to-follow graphics that allow you to work out your own Rising Sign, and that of anyone whose time of birth you know. You will find instructions on using the graphics on page 129.

Happy hunting – and remember: the more you know about a person, the greater your ability to get on well with them. That's what relationships are about. Whether you are dealing with friendship, business associations, family ties or romance, *Build Better Zodiac Relationships* can be your invaluable guide to getting on well with others.

Chapter 1
Aries
21 March to 20 April

 ARIES meets ARIES

The meeting of Aries with Aries is always going to be a reactive and probably very interesting coming-together. Aries is the most dynamic, forthright and fiery of all the zodiac signs. In almost any situation, Aries people rise to the fore and are the individuals to whom others instinctively look for leadership. Put two of them together and there are often strong reactions, because neither wishes to back down and both want to rule the roost.

There are saving graces, of course. It can be very satisfying to know exactly what to expect from another person, and particularly so in a romantic attachment. There should also be a great mutual regard and probably an increased tendency for reactive Aries to temper its usual overly direct approach. But if it's action you want, there will be no shortage of that.

Most importantly of all, this meeting breeds some friction in all practical matters and financial ventures, and to get the greatest benefits from this, you must ensure an early and well-negotiated demarcation of responsibilities. Failure to achieve this objective will undoubtedly lead to confrontation, arguments and a frustrating series of stalemates that will not suit anyone, no matter what sort of relationship exists between the two Aries subjects. Communication is the key and, once established, it should help both to realise that exchange of ideas and intentions is vital in any relationship.

When an Aries person meets someone of their own sign in a romantic encounter, the results are apt to be more fruitful than if the relationship is a professional one. The reason for this lies in what Aries thinks of itself. After all, if you are generally satisfied with your own personality, you can hardly fail to find comfort and excitement when constantly faced with someone whose presence is akin to looking in a mirror. All the same, you should be prepared for some very definite and often prolonged fireworks.

ARIES meets TAURUS

In any sort of association between these two zodiac signs, ground rules are going to be vitally important. Those who don't understand the zodiac well might assume that things are going to be a pushover for fiery, dominant Aries when confronted with the shyer, quieter and more contemplative Taurus individual. Nothing could be further from the truth. It's true that Arians have much more to say for themselves and are naturally more ambitious and self-motivated, but we all know what happens when an irresistible force meets an immovable object . . .

The ultimate results are really down to the Aries individual here. It is possible to get kind, compassionate and practical Taurus to do almost anything, but certainly not via an aggressive and over-dominant attitude. Subtlety is called for – a commodity that isn't usually to the fore in the case of the Ram. With understanding on both sides, however, the prognosis is actually very good, though it may prove better in professional than in romantic contacts.

Taurus needs its own space and plenty of time to think things through. Aries meanwhile is a go-getting dynamo that relies almost entirely on instinct and instant action. If the essential difference between these two attitudes is reconciled from the word go, then everything in the garden should come up smelling of roses. If it is not, then both parties should prepare themselves for some long silences and a fair degree of misunderstanding. Aries needs to think before it speaks and to listen carefully to what Taurus has to say. When this is done, the result will be strong complementary qualities at work, which could enliven any sort of contact. The only problem may be that Aries and Taurus may discover with the passing of time that they have very little in common. This is especially true in social situations.

With this combination of signs, however, nothing is impossible. With a good long chat at the start of the relationship, you could be looking at the makings of a mutual and unique sort of success.

ARIES meets GEMINI

This matching has plenty going for it, and on all sorts of levels. Although born of radically different parts of the zodiac, both the Aries and the Gemini natures contain aspects that can lead to a deep understanding and a mutual appreciation. Aries is inclined to shoot from the hip. It doesn't have the subtlety that is inherent in the sign of Gemini, which is geared more towards mental motivation. This might not be too much of a problem because there are complementary qualities at work. In a professional relationship, for example, Aries can plan the strategies, whilst Gemini can talk the hind leg off a donkey to put them into practice.

Most people assume that Gemini people are superficial. Actually, this is far from being the case, as an unwary Aries individual would soon discover. Gemini people act on intuition, and although they can occasionally come unstuck, their ability to weigh up people and situations can be uncanny. This appeals to the average Aries subject, who may even be envious of this Gemini proclivity. There certainly won't be any lack of things to talk about but both these zodiac signs tend to be independently minded and always want to follow their own course of action. In a long-term personal attachment, this could prove to be something of a problem because, after all, someone has to keep an eye on the children.

The real saving grace here could come through Gemini's ability to adapt, something that Aries is far less able to do. One word of warning, however: Gemini people can be very untidy and have butterfly minds to match, whilst Arians are more centred and determined, usually concentrating all their attention on just one thing at a time. Despite this, there is great potential for success when Aries and Gemini come together in any kind of relationship. Certainly life should be interesting for them, even if a little exasperating for the Aries half of the attachment. Arians tend to be naturally protective of Gemini people, who in return have the ability to make the Rams more inclined to laugh at themselves. One thing they have in common: both these zodiac signs are happy to flout rules.

 ## ARIES meets CANCER

There is a good chance that almost any Aries subject will find an instant rapport with the much quieter and more contemplative zodiac sign of Cancer. Of course it must be borne in mind that Aries is a Fire sign, whilst the element that rules Cancer is Water. To an astrologer this speaks instantly of a potentially 'steamy' relationship – though this need not necessarily prove to be a bad thing. Arians are chock-full of ego, whilst it often seems on the surface that the average Cancerian subject has none at all. Nevertheless, Cancer people are not averse to positive individuals and often choose their company.

What we are looking at here is a quite dramatic coming-together of opposites, which, paradoxically, is rarely a recipe for disaster. In any sort of relationship, Cancer can rely heavily on the dynamic qualities inherent in the Ram, whilst Arians can find in the Crab a quieter and more contemplative quality that they desperately need but rarely discover within themselves. In short, Aries will speed up Cancer, whilst Cancer imposes a less intense sense of urgency on Aries.

Both these zodiac signs are often found in the caring professions, though usually for radically different reasons. Aries subjects tend towards surgery and make good doctors, whilst Cancer breeds natural nurses. However, this fact does show that they can both represent good homemakers when they come together. Arians should exercise some care because they tend to dominate without realising. Cancerians, meanwhile, are inclined to say nothing about this tendency for months on end, until finally they explode. So beware, Aries, if your Cancerian lover or workmate is quiet and brooding towards you for any length of time, you may well have upset them in some way and need to talk things through. Somehow that's much easier for you to do in the case of Cancer than with almost any other zodiac sign.

It can be difficult to understand why radically different people find common ground, but in the case of Aries and Cancer they often do.

 ## ARIES meets LEO

This is an all-or-nothing match that will send sparks flying in all directions. From the start, no matter what the nature of the attachment, you must realise that both Aries and Leo are Fire signs of the most dynamic sort. The ways they manifest this quality to the world at large are rather different, but that doesn't mean that either the Ram or the Lion is likely to be bossed around by anyone. It might even be fair to suggest that when Aries and Leo come together there is either an immediate natural liking or an instantaneous loathing.

On the negative side, both zodiac signs have a natural tendency to want to be in charge. Of course, that isn't always possible and so there are bound to be occasions when one or other of these individuals will have to back down. Nevertheless, as long as each recognises that they possess skills and proclivities that are different from the other's, some break-even point can be established. Under almost all circumstances Leos will cheer up Aries, simply because they have a sunnier and more optimistic nature. Leos are bold and fearless, and can be incredibly kind – all qualities that are certain to appeal to the rather more aloof, but equally aspiring, Aries individual.

The association of Aries and Leo should certainly carry potential success in a financial sense. Both are good earners and don't shy away from hard work. Both have good administrative abilities and can make things happen, even against all the odds.

Confrontation should be avoided, though you must accept that it's going to happen occasionally, whether this is a friendship, a family tie or a romance. An agreement to differ can help, as will a readiness on both sides to admit that nobody has a monopoly on being in the right.

To make this relationship work, it's necessary to put away the swords and the spears and to realise that even people of an extremely dynamic sort can achieve a rapport. There needs to be a willingness on both parts to listen and not merely a desire to browbeat others into following one's own point of view. If this is understood, the sky is the limit for Aries in its association with Leo.

 ## ARIES meets VIRGO

It has often been suggested that when Fire signs and Earth signs come together things get done, and that does appear to be the case with Aries and Virgo. The only small fly in the ointment may be that, although very different in almost every other way, Aries and Virgo are both self-centred zodiac signs. Each has its own objectives and both expect other people to come on board and help out. If everyone has the same desires and objectives, then all should be well. Sadly, this will not always prove to be the case.

Aries is frank, free, outspoken, dominant and sometimes overbearing. Virgo, meanwhile, is apparently outgoing but at the same time deeply insular. Virgo gets round other people, not through dynamism, but by dogged persistence and sometimes – let's face it – by nagging. This latter tendency doesn't suit Aries at all and is inclined to be a source of friction if not fully understood by both parties. A good dollop of communication is required here, as is a willingness on the part of both individuals to realise that there are many different ways of living one's life.

In business attachments and where family ties are concerned, we have little choice as to the nature of the people with whom we are thrown together, so you may find that the Aries–Virgo combination arises here. Personal attachments are a different kettle of fish, however, and it seems to be the case that Aries and Virgo are less likely to come together under these circumstances.

In some respects, the gap between Aries and Virgo is a little too wide. Virgo people daydream, whilst Aries people generally don't. In addition, those born under the sign of the Virgin are inclined to worry about almost everything. Having a go-getting, dominant and perhaps risk-taking Aries partner around all the time probably won't alleviate this tendency, but it may toughen up the Virgoan mental state and lead to a willingness to take a few chances, some of which could lead to a greater sense of fulfilment.

The differences between these two are therefore not insurmountable, and such relationships can certainly be good for all materialistic considerations.

ARIES meets LIBRA

The Aries zodiac sign is ruled by the fiery and dynamic planet Mars, whereas Libra, the diplomat of the stars, responds to serene Venus. There could hardly be two people less alike, a factor that might lead us to believe that this is the mismatch to beat them all. In reality, however, this really isn't the case. It is a fundamental fact in magnetism that opposites attract and this also often turns out to be the case with Aries and Libra. The reason for this isn't particularly profound: what Aries needs, Libra can provide, whilst those traits of nature missing from the sign of the Scales are readily to be found in that of the Ram.

Prolonged periods in the company of urbane, sociable and friendly Libra are apt to knock some of the more feisty edges off Aries people and cause them to look again at their own tendency to fire indiscriminately in all directions. Meanwhile, Librans, who are often far too laid-back for their own good, have important lessons in assertiveness to learn from the most progressive sign around. In a business partnership, the balance of Libra adds a more 'human' dimension to the success that Aries seeks, and also tempers the desire of the Ram to get where it needs to be, sometimes at any cost.

Personal relationships between these two signs benefit from a variety of different stimuli. Aries individuals find Librans easy-going and are inclined to show their own most romantic qualities as a result. Secure family ties often result, and a commitment to progress that is both strong and sustained. A Libran knows how to smooth the stress wrinkles from the Aries brow and can be of tremendous assistance when it comes to offering alternative initiatives and fresh ideas. Creature comforts are important, but not absolutely essential, to both signs – so this also provides a meeting-point.

All in all, Aries and Libra may not appear to be absolutely made for each other but in some instances, this may, indeed, be the case.

ARIES meets SCORPIO

There are gains to be found from this pairing, in terms of friendship, business and romance, that stem from the fact that both these zodiac signs are ruled by Mars. The planet displays itself quite differently in each case, though its presence does allow bridges to be built that might otherwise be difficult.

Aries needs to be in charge, whilst Scorpio really doesn't respond to being told what to do by anyone. In any relationship setting, this will always provide the potential for some heated arguments, though these could quite easily lead to a greater common respect – if someone doesn't get killed on the way!

Scorpio is deeper and more sensitive than Aries, and so is more likely to take any sort of disagreement to heart. Scorpio is also capable of sulking, which is far less likely in the case of Aries. In a work situation, things work out better if the Ram is handing out the orders and the Scorpion is the one following them. Caution is necessary, however, because there can be friction if the Scorpion concerned disagrees with either the instruction itself, or the way it must be carried out.

Pairs of siblings born of these two zodiac signs are apt to fight most of the time, except when faced with a common foe, in which case they stick together and can defeat almost any enemy. In romantic entanglements, the coming-together of Aries and Scorpio really shows its true potential. There is deep sensuality coming from Scorpio, which is perfectly matched to the Aries determination to prove itself the world's best lover. Those involved in this match can develop a profound and sincere attachment but are still likely to disagree on many occasions. The resulting shouting matches will probably be heard three streets away, though both these zodiac signs being what they are, the potential for making up ought to be excellent.

Interestingly, Arians are not as sure of themselves as they often appear, whilst Scorpio is also inclined to be lacking in self-confidence. Together, however, both signs can be stronger.

 ## ARIES meets SAGITTARIUS

This is a pairing that needs to remain fairly superficial. It could hardly be otherwise, since neither of these zodiac signs tends to throw up profound thinkers. Aries and Sagittarius individuals make good and often lifelong friends; neither will make massive demands on the other and they share a common understanding that makes time spent together happy and undemanding. But because both Aries and Sagittarius are Fire signs there is almost certain to be some jockeying for position, no matter what the nature of the relationship. If an open competition develops, it is likely that Aries will come out on top, though something important may be lost on the way.

Those born under Sagittarius, the sign of the Archer, are quick to fire off arrows of observation and wit. These generally find their mark, and the degree of sarcasm sometimes used won't particularly please an Aries subject who happens to be the target. As a rule Aries doesn't have quite what it takes to respond in kind and this can lead to a degree of frustration that the Ram simply will not enjoy. The key to harmony in this relationship is plenty of communication and a deeper understanding on the part of Aries as to the way Sagittarius functions.

This is another very reactive relationship if it exists on a personal or romantic level. Both these zodiac signs can love with a passion, despite the fact that Sagittarius is less inclined to be loyal in the long term if the romance isn't offering constant change and interest. Arians are more staunch in their affections and can sometimes fall foul of the Archer's tendency to seek out fresh fields and pastures new.

Maybe the best area for this association is within the realms of work. If an Aries and a Sagittarian are both typical of their zodiac signs, they can form a business partnership that is almost certain to succeed. Aries will do the organising and promoting, whilst Sagittarius will be out in the marketplace, doing the selling. Both these Fire signs are extremely hard workers.

ARIES meets CAPRICORN

This may not be at all a bad pairing, though it is apt to look somewhat one-sided when viewed through the eyes of outsiders. Aries wants everything immediately, if not yesterday, whilst Capricorn is quite willing to wait and will work long and hard to achieve its desired objectives. Capricorn people are definitely slower than Aries in every way. This means that the Ram is almost always the one to make the running and is constantly urging the Goat to catch up. However, as in the story of the tortoise and the hare, it isn't necessarily Aries who will reach the winning post first.

This association could well be good for business. Arians are full of bright, new ideas and initiatives. They may not care for the way Capricorn goes about putting them into practice but can at least take solace from the fact that the job will be done completely – and well. Capricorn, meanwhile, isn't all that worried about making all the decisions and is usually happy to follow the leader. This does not mean that the Goat can be browbeaten or bullied by Aries, however – Capricorn does not respond well to any form of coercion.

Undoubtedly there are romantically tied Aries and Capricorn subjects who live together in perfect harmony, but Capricorn certainly isn't the most common choice to complement the sign of the Ram. The fact is that, despite superficial similarities, Goats and Rams are really very different creatures: they don't inhabit the same terrain and have different diets – especially from an emotional point of view. All the same, this could be a fantastic recipe for friendship or business success, and any sort of relationship may prosper if the Capricorn individual is of the more flexible type.

The most evident aspect of this relationship is a sort of mutual respect that outsiders might wonder at. Aries and Capricorn people have much more in common than may be immediately obvious, for despite views to the contrary, in their own way both zodiac signs are quite ruthless.

ARIES meets AQUARIUS

Aquarius is one sign of the zodiac where Arians are likely not only to meet their match, but to be bettered. At first sight they really don't have much in common – nor at second or third sight, for that matter. Aquarian individuals rely extremely heavily on intuition, a word and an ability that are virtually unknown to the average Aries subject. Aquarians wish to know not only how certain things work in the world but also why. The latter is of far less interest to Aries, who would consider departures into the very philosophical workings of the universe to be something of a waste of time.

Things may turn out well in certain circumstances, if only because Aquarius is an Air sign and therefore incredibly adaptable. Staying-power, however, except in family situations where there is little choice, is not often in evidence. Like Aries, Aquarius enjoys being on the move, but is also inclined to stop at every ford and hill to survey the landscape of life, a mode of action that would be quite lost on ambitious Aries, who simply wants to arrive at the next destination. In a marital situation, there will almost certainly be radically different ideas of how children should be raised and also quite different views concerning their long-term future. Nevertheless, both signs are distinctly family-minded and make excellent parents.

Both these zodiac signs tend to be extremely opinionated, although Aquarius shows the fact less in open argument. Aquarius is very much geared towards the future and to any explanations and revelations that it holds in store. This is a sign that genuinely cares about the wallpaper of life, something that Aries individuals don't notice at all.

In cases where the attachment does work romantically, it is likely to be quirky, erratic and extremely unorthodox. Note the couple in the pub who wear radically different clothes and who rarely agree about any detail of life, but who go home arm-in-arm – still disagreeing. They could well be an Aries and an Aquarian.

 # ARIES meets PISCES

Almost any astrologer who has mixed with people for a number of years and observed their behaviour at close quarters will tell you that Aries and Pisces people quite often do get together. This is strange in a way, because Aries is usually noisy, adventurous, risk-taking and bold. Pisceans, on the other hand, are insular, quiet, rarely inclined to make waves and often specifically dedicated to offering themselves to humanity as a whole.

It may well be that the protective arm offered by Aries seems to be particularly welcoming to the average Pisces. Pisceans are impressed with strength and support, though in a romantic attachment this can, with the passing of time, seem stifling and less than welcome. Aries people who find themselves tied to Pisceans need to forge a more understanding attitude and to allow a great deal of leeway to a zodiac sign that is so deep it cannot even fathom its own depths.

Aries individuals have much to offer the world. They are filled with potential of all kinds. Intuitive Pisces recognises this fact and is certain to be impressed by it. The sign of the Ram can be toned down and caressed by the presence of Pisces. However, rather than taking the edge off the tough Aries nature, this is inclined to encourage it to work that much better. A greater degree of understanding of humanity is the basic lesson that Aries needs to learn the most.

In family relationships, the Aries individual will almost always prove to be the more dominant. Pisceans are not half so sure of themselves and will usually defer to the opinions, ideas and initiatives put forward by the Ram. Friendship and romance are slightly different ballgames, since neither is likely to start to develop unless both parties feel that, at some level, they are each gaining something from the attachment. When they are, there can be a good deal of mutual hero-worship.

If this attachment is cemented early in life, it may well endure for a very long time.

Chapter 2
Taurus

21 April to 21 May

 TAURUS meets ARIES

To be suddenly thrust into the presence of an individual as driving, dynamic and even domineering as an archetypal Aries subject can be quite intimidating for some Taureans. Such feelings probably won't last, however, because Taurus, ever practical and itself fairly fearless, won't be impressed for long. The basic Taurean nature isn't particularly moved by power and doesn't easily bow to pressure of any sort. Not that this indicates that any attachment between the two signs would necessarily be either hopeless or difficult. On the contrary, Taurus, which is ruled by Venus, can respond positively to its zodiac neighbour.

Taureans have an innate sense of order and harmony. Invariably this is not the case for Aries, which often responds positively to the organisational skills possessed by the zodiac sign of the Bull. In almost any relationship, the brusque, pushy side of Aries is modified considerably when under the influence of Taurus, which seems to possess some magical hold over the Ram. However, any sort of attachment depends in part on the ability of Aries to get to know a zodiac sign that is very different from its own. Taureans are generally more practical than Aries subjects; they are friendly and anxious to please, something that the Ram finds appealing and attractive.

As far as friendship is concerned, these individuals will generally be brought together by circumstances beyond their own immediate control, for Aries and Taurus tend to enjoy different sorts of social life. Once the bond is forged, however, each may make modifications and a number of shared interests may develop. Taurus does need reassurance, which isn't always forthcoming from ever-busy Aries, who can sometimes come across as being a little thoughtless.

Taurus, though diplomatic, is not afraid to speak its mind, whilst Aries is very reactive, and so things are not always plain sailing between the two, particularly when they are involved in any sort of romantic attachment. Nevertheless, with a little give and take on both sides, the prognosis need not be bad. Aries offers hard work, a protecting arm and good earning potential; Taurus is a homemaker and patient to a fault.

This is a combination that can succeed.

 ## TAURUS meets TAURUS

Most individuals find that it is relatively easy to get on with people from their own zodiac sign. There are exceptions but Taurus is not one of them. The reason is that Taureans love a simple and uncomplicated life. Patient, caring but nevertheless very strong, Taureans are not inclined to argue unless they find themselves faced with individuals who try to take advantage of them in some way. Another Taurean is less likely than most to cross the Bull's threshold and as a result there simply isn't anything to argue about.

There is a negative side to the instant liking that takes place between Taureans, however, mainly born out of the fact that too much similarity is apt to lead to a degree of boredom. Taureans may not enjoy disharmony or arguments, but such situations keep them on their toes and allow the more assertive qualities of Taurus to rise to the surface. It's a fact that Taureans can sometimes be lazy, so that two Bulls together may not have enough incentive to push forward in life.

There is certainly no lack of loyalty, courage and support in this pairing, no matter at what level it exists, and this is even more obvious when romance is the motivating factor. Taureans are quite happy in settled relationships. Two together will be more than doubly content. There is mutual support here and a gigantic commitment to home and family. But there may be dullness too, together with an inability to strive for new horizons. In the fullness of time, this could create a fairly sedentary structure to the relationship, which should be constantly enlivened by both parties. Fresh fields and pastures new are an essential component of any Taurus–Taurus attachment and the parties concerned definitely do need to spend time in the company of very different astrological types. This may not be easy because there is an inherent desire for stability and security that seems to be best served by remaining at home with someone who is known and trusted.

Confidence is absolutely essential to Taurus and it might not be readily found when there are too many Bulls in the same stall.

TAURUS meets GEMINI

This is a relationship that works extremely well at almost any level. Taureans are very likeable people, even if their stubbornness is something of a problem to some, and one sign of the zodiac that definitely doesn't find Taurus difficult to deal with is Gemini. This might have something to do with the Gemini nature, which is variable, adaptable and tolerant. It's true that with this pairing Gemini is likely to do most of the talking but this may suit the average Taurean quite well, and in any case having a Gemini chatterbox about will enliven even the most reserved Taurus individual.

Taurean practicality is important to Gemini types, who are disorganised and inclined to forget even the most important details when left to their own devices. This certainly is not the case with Taureans, who, like elephants, never forget. Taurus loves to receive compliments, which Gemini is only too willing to supply. Practically the only fly in the ointment is that Gemini is capricious and almost certainly not as loyal as Taurus. If the relationship exists on a personal and a romantic level, stay-at-home Taurus may soon get exasperated with Gemini, who always wants to be on the go.

Long-term relationships made up from this zodiac sign combination very rarely go stale. Gemini forces Taurus to take on a greater role in the world at large, whilst Taurus offers a degree of stability that Gemini might sometimes push against, but which it definitely needs.

Children born of such relationships can expect a stable but sometimes unorthodox upbringing and a range of advice and experience that would appear to fit them for practically any station in life. Both these zodiac signs are naturally kind and pleasant by nature. They will have many friends in common and will enjoy financial and material success.

Gemini individuals may be fickle but they tend to be hard workers with the practical aspects of Taurus to nudge them along. Taurus, meanwhile, gains from the sheer diversity and confidence-building qualities of Gemini.

 # TAURUS meets CANCER

Whether these individuals are just good friends, or a couple who have been together for many years, they should hardly be expected to create a stir. Both Taurus and Cancer are what are known as 'negative' zodiac signs. This merely means that they tend, on balance, to be introverted. It is perhaps for this reason that the matching of Taurus and Cancer, at least at a romantic level, is not really all that common. Certainly this will be a placid, mutually kind and considerate attachment.

People born under these zodiac signs can be expected to work together without any real difficulty at all – though it's likely that there will be someone from a much more positive part of the zodiac pulling the strings.

Both Cancer and Taurus are capable of being practical. Cancer is the better homemaker of the pair, though Taurus really isn't too far behind. You probably wouldn't find either at a nightclub – at least not if the decision to go there had been left strictly up to them. Taurus and Cancer would usually rather stay at home, where they create an extremely comfortable environment, though perhaps not one into which too many strangers would stray on a regular basis. Taurus and Cancer are both natural parents, so a large and happy family is very likely.

One should perhaps ask: 'Are these individuals likely to bore each other to death?' The answer lies within the hands of the people concerned. If they recognise that the world is a large and interesting place, and that travel and diversity can broaden the mind, then they can share new experiences together. Carpet slippers should be banned between this pair, and the money saved spent on whooping it up now and again.

Taurus and Cancer may not provide the most exciting relationships in the world. However, with harmony in abundance and a capacity for great mutual respect and a deep abiding love, it would be difficult to criticise the match.

 ## TAURUS meets LEO

Taureans are like sponges and tend to soak up any sort of influence that predominates in their lives. That's part of the reason why they are so happy and respond so positively to the presence of the zodiac sign of Leo. People born under the sign of the Lion are usually cheerful. Leos have a warm disposition, and are frank, fearless and loyal. All of these qualities have a special appeal to Taurus, who has an instinctive liking for the best of what Leo often turns out to be. Taureans and Leos make good workmates and since Leo also has the ability to bring out the funny side of Taurus, there are usually plenty of laughs to be had when this pair are around.

It's true that Leo can sometimes be a little overbearing, though Taurus doesn't usually notice the fact. The only real potential drawback may lie in the inborn, stubborn streak that the Bull possesses. Leos like to get their own way, whilst Taureans refuse to be budged once they have set their minds to any particular course of action. In the main, however, arguments between this pair should be few and a meeting of minds easy to achieve.

Leos like the high life though, like the lion that they represent, they intersperse this with long periods of idleness. In the main this won't worry Taureans at all, since they also have a great capacity for rest and relaxation.

On the other hand, Leo retains an ability to talk Taurus into experiences that it might not otherwise contemplate, broadening the Bull's horizons and making for a more interesting life generally.

Both these zodiac signs are family-minded and each can contribute their own valuable qualities to common objectives. Taurus is ruled by passive Venus, whilst Leo responds to the much more dynamic qualities of the Sun. The two together can discover a balance that should be comfortable for both parties. Taureans are also much friendlier characters when Leo is around and will discover more about themselves when in the company of the Lion.

 TAURUS meets VIRGO

It has to be said from the very outset that this is not likely to be the most dynamic or inspiring pairing to be found within the zodiac. Both Taurus and Virgo are born under the Earth element. This means that, at heart, they are both practical and inclined to stick to what they know. Virgo has the greater curiosity of the two signs and also might be the chattier. Unfortunately Virgoans are also quite fussy and that might prove to be a problem. Whether at work, in situations of friendship or in deeper commitments, there are aspects of Taurus and Virgo that are simply too similar. This can lead to some friction because although the desire to organise is present in both cases, the ways of achieving it differ markedly.

If the problems of demarcation can be sorted out amicably, Taurus and Virgo can live together in some sort of harmony, even if a certain 'spark' is apt to be missing. Actually this may only be a problem when viewed through the eyes of other, more dynamic zodiac sign types, since Taurus and Virgo are both happy to settle for a fairly quiet life. As a couple, Taurus and Virgo need mutual friends, from different parts of the zodiac wheel. Both signs are refined and love clean, uncluttered surroundings. Virgo is naturally more neurotic than Taurus, who can act as a stabilising influence to the slightly 'wonky' Virgoan nervous system. Virgo repays this favour by offering Taurus every snippet of information that comes its way.

Both these zodiac signs are very good at making money and are not averse to hard work. With both their incentives and generally their actions in common, only a desire to be perpetually in charge of any given situation will force a wedge between this pair.

Life may be settled between Taurus and Virgo – but is it genuinely interesting? If the answer to the question turns out to be a very definite 'No', it will most likely be left up to Virgo to find ways to bring inspiration and interest into the relationship. All that is really needed is some excitement – and this can be provided quite simply, for example by way of travel.

TAURUS meets LIBRA

There are several very good reasons why this match is a particularly good one. For a start, both these zodiac signs are ruled by the planet Venus. That alone means that Taurus and Libra have a great deal in common, though they are also different enough to allow an element of 'spice' to come into the pairing too. It is a fact that in a business association Libra is likely to be more outgoing, more ambitious and even somewhat more adaptable than Taurus. This won't be too much of a problem though, because Taurus brings a more rigid attention to detail and a sense of ultimate purpose that Libra is inclined to lack.

In the family, Taurus and Libra make a very good match. Both are loyal, enjoy the same things and can make each other laugh. Libra is the natural diplomat and also has the ability to deal with the stubborn streaks that Taurus sometimes exhibits. Both signs are, in any case, loyal and entertaining family members and are inclined to shower affection on those they care for.

Best of all is romance. Taurus and Libra are never short of something to say to each other. Their sense of romance is more or less the same, even if Libra tends to be somewhat more capricious and fickle. Both these zodiac signs are quite happy to have a good time, each is quite artistic and refined, and their views of relationships are shared. Socially speaking, those born under the Bull and the Scales are likely to turn heads, though they are inclined to do so in a fairly low-key sort of way. There is no embarrassment felt by either party at the antics of the other and they share a common desire to have an ordered and tidy household.

If there is a downside, it might be that the home of these characters could be too tidy and that these particular zodiac signs, when working together, may be trying to create what amounts to a palace, rather than a home. All in all, however, Libra represents one of the best associations that Taurus could enjoy at any level.

 ## TAURUS meets SCORPIO

There is one factor in the Taurus–Scorpio match that has to be considered at every level. I am referring to the fact that both are what is known as 'fixed' zodiac signs. Generally speaking, this means that each is capable of being extremely stubborn on occasions. As long as things are going well and both parties are happy with life, that won't be a problem. The difficulty comes when one has decided to do one thing, whilst the other has its heart set on something else. In every case, from a simple friendship, right through to the most intense love affair, difficulties can be avoided if both simply avoid their tendency to dig their heels in.

Once this advice has been taken on board, the match is not at all a difficult one. Both Taurus and Scorpio know the value of loyalty and both can be quite 'deep' on occasions. This could make for a fairly quiet attachment, though Taurus is certainly more inclined to chat than the Scorpion. The Bull has the same problem as anyone dealing with the Scorpio individual – namely, trying to understand the internal thought processes of such an intense person – though Taurus is likely to deal with the situation better than most. Financially speaking, both signs are good workers and can contribute very well to a common desire to bring in the money.

A personal relationship built around these two signs can easily be very steamy at times, with the accent on in-depth feelings rather than any frothy sort of romance, which neither would particularly enjoy. Both signs are fiercely defensive of loved ones and especially younger family members. Family and personal routines will be dealt with in similar ways, though efforts will have to be made frequently to ring the changes, in order to avoid a sense of staleness or even boredom creeping in. If marriage is on the cards, the engagement may be a fairly protracted one, but the final celebrations will be wonderful to behold in their efficiency, scale and complexity.

On the whole, Taurus and Scorpio do get on very well together.

TAURUS meets SAGITTARIUS

It's hard to fall out with the zany, capricious, tricky and sometimes even duplicitous Sagittarian. The majority of the other signs of the zodiac find the Archer especially attractive and Taurus is no exception. Some problems can arise when the Sagittarians' natural tendency to do their own thing at all costs suddenly manifests itself – Taurus likes routine and doesn't take kindly to changing direction at a moment's notice. Once again, this indicates the 'fixed' quality of the Taurean nature, which exists in startling contrast to the mutable qualities inherent in Sagittarius.

Very few problems fail to carry a gift in their arms in one way or another, however. Sagittarius does sometimes need to concentrate more and to show a greater sense of responsibility and Taurus can benefit from loosening up a little. Since even at the level of simple friendship, some cross-fertilisation is almost certain to take place between the Bull and the Archer, these zodiac signs can be very good for each other. Between any two extremes there is an average, and that's what Taurus and Sagittarius together can achieve.

Neither of these types is inclined to compromise very much, even if Sagittarians spend half their lives pretending that they do so all the time.

Perhaps that isn't too important because each party in this coming-together has natural gifts to offer that will be appreciated by the other. There will be friendliness, laughter and enjoyment in this liaison, with Sagittarius bringing much fun too. Some of the constraints of the Taurean nature are blown away on the breeze of the Archer's natural affability and zany sense of humour.

The match can be occasionally uncomfortable for the laid-back Bull because Sagittarius rarely stays still for long and is unlikely to spend two weeks cooking on a foreign beach with a good book. Movement is the key and the Bull will have to come to terms with this fact if Sagittarius is not to be seen leaping off into the distance.

TAURUS meets CAPRICORN

This is essentially a very practical pairing. The most important point of a meeting between Taurus and Capricorn is in the fact that they both respond to the Earth element. In a nutshell, this means that both signs get things done. A sort of no-nonsense approach to life is forged by the Bull and the Goat when they are brought together, whether through a family tie or perhaps as a result of work. Neither sign is particularly progressive, except in a slow and steady way, so this alliance won't set the world on fire. Nevertheless, with plodding but marked determination, and a definite ability to look and plan ahead, Taurus and Capricorn can move massive mountains in the fullness of time.

Both these zodiac signs can be trusted to function without too much supervision and when working together, lines of demarcation will be laid quite naturally. We can expect little in the way of friction or conflict, even if the association isn't exactly inspirational. Both these Earth signs work at their best when some challenge comes their way. This usually happens because of their interaction with more progressive members of the zodiac family and when this is absent there could be a lacklustre aspect to some areas of life and work.

This is not an especially common romantic match. At the most basic level, Taurus and Capricorn are not likely to cement a personal alliance, simply because neither sign is of the type inclined to make the running. If, against the odds, the Bull and Goat are thrust together, the outlook for the future is mixed. Certainly this would be a peaceful household, if not an especially inspiring one. The abode of these individuals will probably be clean and tidy, with an enlightened and cultured atmosphere predominating most of the time. Household chores will probably be shared equally and responsibilities towards family will also be held in common.

The main pitfall in this relationship may be that there is little chance of any spark of individuality, spontaneity or even sheer fun to be present.

TAURUS meets AQUARIUS

The motivating factor in this combination comes not specifically from Taurus itself, but from its association with the much more idiosyncratic zodiac sign of Aquarius. Taurus is steady, serene, cultured and also stubborn. Aquarius understands these qualities but is also far more reactive and quirky. The presence of a typical Aquarian character comes as a wake-up call to the Bull and frees some of the deeper aspirations and qualities that it keeps hidden. Taurus loves the capricious quality of Aquarius and even the fact that people born under this zodiac sign are not easy to pigeon-hole. The Bull would look towards Aquarius for advice on matters of all kinds, even though Taurus itself probably has far more common sense. However, when compared with Aquarius, it does lack genuine self-confidence and an ability to make instant decisions.

Taurus works well with almost any sign of the zodiac, though its association with Aquarius in work situations should be particularly lively and enjoyable. Aquarius can make Taurus laugh, and that's an important factor in any association between these two individuals. Romance is highly likely with this combination. Aquarius longs for the personal common sense and stability that Taurus possesses in abundance. On the way, Taurus gains through constantly having fresh fields and pastures new to consider. Aquarians keep Taureans on their toes and prevent any semblance of Earth-sign lethargy creeping in.

The association of Taurus and Aquarius can also be extremely good on a financial level. Here we find just the right sort of combination to conceive potentially rewarding strategies, then to put them in place and follow them through to their conclusion. On the way there are many jokes, hundreds of cuddles and a wealth of new experiences for this lucky pair to share. Aquarius will also bring many friends into the equation and help Taureans to fulfil their natural but latent desire for travel. Aquarius is also more steadfast when cemented into a relationship with Taurus.

 ## TAURUS meets PISCES

There is a great deal of depth in this matching, probably too much for most practical purposes. Taurus is a very reflective sign and is much altered by its association with others. This mirror-like quality is fine when Taurus is gazing at some of the more positive zodiac signs but less so with Pisces – simply because no reflection comes back. Pisces is friendly, generous to a fault and extremely kind, but not easy to understand. Taurus meanwhile, being an

Earth sign and showing a response to languorous Venus, can be quite lazy at times. Herein lies a potential problem because, at any relationship level, the Bull may not care to attempt to plumb the depths of the Piscean pool.

There is hardly likely to be much animosity generated in this relationship, so Taurus and Pisces can both work and live together in harmony. They each exhibit a great deal of kindness and understanding and may develop a lifelong attachment of sorts. A mutual respect is likely, as is the ability to build common objectives. What may be missing is that certain 'something' that comes from rubbing up against a character who is radically different from oneself. If both these individuals are typical of the zodiac signs into which they were born, the prognosis for a kind of contentment is good, but much of what can make both Taurus and Pisces fulfilled may be missing. These facts may only be registered as a sort of subconscious 'emptiness' and, in some cases, will be dismissed almost instantly.

On a romantic level, Taurus and Pisces make for a very sympathetic liaison. Seen from the outside, these individuals can be viewed as kind and loving, with a distinctly demonstrative quality, particularly from the direction of Pisces. Economic success may be possible, mainly thanks to Taurus, and the pair will gain greatly from an ability to search out new horizons whenever possible. They may prefer a staid and steady life but that could lead to a certain degree of tedium. Routines are to be avoided wherever possible, especially in the long term. A change is as good as a rest and particularly so when Taurus and Pisces come together.

Chapter 3
Gemini
22 May to 21 June

 GEMINI meets ARIES

Gemini is one of the most adaptable signs of the zodiac and as a result it has a potential for relationships with almost any other sign. That said, some are likely to be more successful than others and the Gemini–Aries contact is probably one of these. Gemini people are naturally inclined to be intuitive, a quality that is greatly admired by Aries. The Ram is likely to act on impulse and does not possess Gemini's ability to weigh up the pros and cons of situations or the potential within individuals. Conversely, those born under the sign of the Twins often find themselves unable to follow their actions through, an ability that comes as second nature to Aries. Thus we find an immediate ability for the two zodiac signs to complement each other and to work towards common objectives, each using their own respective capabilities.

The very ability of Gemini to change itself to suit prevailing circumstances means that the sometimes brusque and even domineering qualities of Aries are less of a problem here. Gemini respects single-mindedness, probably because it is weak in this department. In addition its ability to talk fluently and convincingly on just about any subject appeal greatly to the Ram. Gemini often plans whilst Aries does, and this suits all concerned.

On a personal level, the prognosis is also fairly good. Both signs are progressive and each is a 'positive' zodiac sign. Neither is a stay-at-home type and Aries can supply the potential for adventure that is so important to Gemini. Expect a reactive relationship. Any arguments are likely to be sharp and vitriolic – but they won't last long and though Arians can bear a grudge with the best of them, they are less likely to do so in this case. Family considerations may take something of a back seat but there isn't much doubt that this pair are headed for excitement and financial success – if they don't bankrupt themselves in the first six months. Gemini especially needs diversity and change, which Aries is also happy to supply.

GEMINI meets TAURUS

There are times when Taurus can seem like a real stick-in-the-mud. After all, its sign symbol is the steady, plodding, determined Bull. Taurus is also a 'fixed' zodiac sign, so it doesn't necessarily adapt to circumstances that go against the grain. However, if there is one zodiac sign that can almost always bring out the best in Taurus, it is Gemini. There is an instinctive understanding between these two zodiac signs that any professional astrologer is likely to have seen working well time and time again. It may be born of the fact that Gemini is so charming, for Taurus is inordinately vain, whilst at the same time lacking in basic self-appreciation. Gemini is able to bolster the nature of the Bull, allowing its latent confidence to shine through and bringing happiness to the average Taurean individual.

Gemini is caring, even if it turns out to be in a superficial way. The sign is said to be fickle, and this accusation contains more than a grain of truth, although there are exceptions in combinations with certain zodiac signs. Taurus is one of these, maybe because those born under the sign of the Bull are so willing to help Gemini play out its strategies and fantasies in the real world. Taurus brings a solidity that Gemini often lacks and it can take a Gemini inspiration or idea and work hard with it until it becomes a reality. Taurus is also very romantic by nature and responds well to the string of compliments that fly from the tongue of the average Gemini. Taureans may realise that Gemini is over-egging the pudding, but they probably don't care.

Continuity is part of the Taurean legacy and it is useful to Gemini, to whom immediacy is often too much a way of life. As a result, a natural balance is achieved, with Gemini lightening the load of plodding Taurus, and the Bull preventing Gemini from flying so high its wings are burned. A deep and abiding attachment can develop here, and this is a union that looks outward to the world. This couple will have many dear friends and will probably relish any potential for travel. Changes do have to be made for the sake of Gemini but Taurus can deal with them well.

 ## GEMINI meets GEMINI

When Gemini meets Gemini, the two signs get on but usually only on a superficial level. The sign of the Twins definitely works at its very best when it has to accommodate personalities different from its own, if only because it has chameleon-like qualities itself. Trying to discover what really makes Gemini tick is like attempting to hold the wind in your hand. When two Geminis come together, particularly at a personal level, there is a lack of fixedness and an inability to grasp something essential in an opposing or complementary nature.

It isn't all bad of course, and in some cases it is positively good. Friendships between Gemini subjects are usually joyful encounters, full of action, verve, eloquence and entertainment. Two actors are certainly better than one for any production, and since Gemini people are acting their parts on the stage of life for most of the time, this two-hander is usually fun for everyone around. This includes the Gemini individuals themselves – but only up to a point. Gemini subjects lack personal cohesion and they require the stability that comes from centring themselves on individuals with a greater sense of commitment and purpose. This can definitely be missing when two Geminis meet and the result is often a charming but inevitable confusion.

When it comes to long-term personal relationships, this is an encounter that begins in a maelstrom of mutual appreciation. Compliments will come thick and fast and romance will spark like an electric storm. However, someone has to see to paying the bills and doing the washing-up, neither of which is a task that those born under the sign of the Twins relish very much. If this pair can work hard to discover their lines of demarcation, then all can be well, but this often turns out not to be the case. Arguments are few and far between, though discontent can arise at many different levels. Fortunately Gemini is the natural talker of the zodiac and so most difficulties can be resolved fairly quickly. It's also a fact that Gemini is incapable of bearing a grudge. Even if things do go wrong, this couple will remain friends.

GEMINI meets CANCER

Cancer is quiet, often very reserved and deep. It is personified by the Crab, which, when trouble threatens, retreats into its shell. If there is one individual who can persuade Cancer to live, freely and willingly, out in the real world, it is Gemini. Cancerians actively like Gemini people, who seem to represent much of what the Crab would wish to be. As with most of us, the sign of Cancer responds well to compliments and in any sort of pairing with Gemini these can be expected to crop up on a regular basis. Cancerians are centred and able to achieve a great deal in the practical world, particularly if they know they are working towards a worthwhile end. Gemini individuals offer the necessary incentives – they act as a Cancerian mouthpiece and protect the vulnerable Crab to the best of their ability.

As workmates, Gemini and Cancer create a happy and carefree environment and one in which a great deal can be done, though not without a good deal of chatter on the way. Even the most insular Cancerian is drawn forth by Gemini, who is generally interested in the way the mind of the Crab works. Ideas flow from Gemini like water from a tap and Cancer has the ability to take these on board and make them work in the real world. Romantically speaking, this ought to be a good match too, for Gemini has just the right words of love to move the Cancerian heart. When the Crab loves, it does so unconditionally, which can occasionally come as a surprise to at least some Geminis, and might even bring a degree of constancy from the Twins that would be missing under other circumstances. In this match Cancerians take on many of the practical tasks, though usually willingly and in the knowledge that their Gemini partners will offer verbal support and, because they are happy, will stay around to help. Activity is the keyword for Gemini, a fact that may sometimes see Cancer becoming exhausted.

This may not be a five-star encounter – but it has the potential to be very close to it. The two signs simply seem to hit it off and that is what counts in the end, even if the reason why is not always exactly clear.

GEMINI meets LEO

This is an encounter filled with joy, unbridled enthusiasm and not a little confusion. The sign of Leo is proud, brave, aspiring and not usually given to being quiet. Gemini is the chatterbox of the zodiac and so when the two come together there is a great deal of talking and a tremendous amount of action to boot. Leo genuinely likes Gemini, at least at first, though it may come to realise that only one in a dozen Gemini ideas actually come to fruition and this could, ultimately, prove to be something of a stumbling-block. Leos, of course, belong to the Fire signs, so they don't generally suffer fools gladly. It has to be said that Gemini is the natural clown of the zodiac, though in this respect the word is used to describe a jester rather than an idiot. When working at its best, Gemini offers the stimulus that turns on the tremendous latent power of the Leo spirit.

As friends, these individuals know where to find fun, and how to create it if it is absent. They tend to form part of a larger group since both Gemini and Leo are very gregarious and love company. There may be times when the two signs upstage each other but both have a tremendous sense of humour and relish a knockabout environment. If the relationship exists at a personal and long-term level, the prognosis is slightly different. Gemini is full of promise, but no individual could possibly achieve everything that the sign of the Twins attempts, with the result that some ideas fall by the wayside. Leo is different. It concentrates less and succeeds where it tries. The Gemini inability to come up with the goods on each and every occasion may sometimes trouble the Lion, and since Gemini has an ego as fragile as eggshells, a certain degree of deflation and disillusionment may follow.

As parents, Gemini and Leo do extremely well. Their family will be one that responds positively to action and to many changes in direction. Children of this match will be taught self-sufficiency and the value of genuine inspiration. They may also be very successful – it's a fact that Gemini and Leo together make extremely good parents.

This relationship is a reactive mix, but that doesn't mean that it is likely to founder.

 ## GEMINI meets VIRGO

Although this match may not be the very best for either party, it does have one saving grace in that both these zodiac signs are ruled by the planet Mercury. This small, speedy planet shows a different face in each case but the common motivation here is the mental attitude that Gemini and Virgo both have. Not that this necessarily shows itself at every level. Virgo is fussy, particular and often very, very careful. Gemini on the other hand is instant, approximate and inclined to rashness, qualities that could ultimately annoy Virgo greatly. However, the sign of the Virgin is by no means immune to the charm of Gemini and probably understands it and responds to it better than most.

Gemini tends to be good for Virgo in almost any sort of association. Virgo instinctively sees in Gemini the more positive side of the Mercurial potential. Virgo has a great tendency to worry, and this can be defused or redirected by the Gemini presence, which inclines Virgo to a greater superficiality – something that it needs very much. Those born under the sign of the Virgin are often inclined to take themselves, and the world, far too seriously. Gemini explodes Virgoan pomposity and lightens its load considerably. On a different level, as we have already seen, Virgo is one of the few zodiac signs that can deeply irritate the usually easy-going Gemini. In a personal attachment, this could eventually be a cause of some frustration. Virgoans will not do anything until they are absolutely ready, whilst those born under the sign of the Twins need to act when the mood takes them. Since nothing, not even the silver tongue of Gemini, can do anything to speed up Virgoan actions, sharp words could ensue.

Gemini and Virgo can achieve shared financial success because each has different gifts to bring to the party. Even riches are not out of the question – that is, if the two parties have not strangled each other before the money really starts rolling in.

This association probably will not be the romance of the century in many cases. There are exceptions to every rule, however, and Mercury-led signs are nothing if not exceptional.

GEMINI meets LIBRA

Here we have a coming-together of two Air signs, which is usually a recipe for eventfulness and action. There is a natural empathy when the Twins and the Scales find each other and also a common purpose – which is mainly to have fun. Experience tells us that those people ruled by Mercury and those under the sway of Venus generally get on together because they complement each other so well. Like two pieces of a jigsaw puzzle, their natures mesh, bringing excitement, understanding and often a deep and abiding affection. This can apply on any level, and since both these signs have many friends and acquaintances, the association is a frequent one.

If there is one thing that Gemini needs more than any other, it is a sense of stability and calm. Libra brings this, though without compromising its own personal need for change and diversity. The twists and turns of life are a source of great interest to Gemini and Libra, who are both great observers and keen travellers. But as the author Robert Louis Stevenson said, 'It is better to travel in hope than to arrive', and it is the journey through life that generates the greatest interest when these zodiac signs come together. At work, this combination is a sure sign that things will happen and that a good deal of inspirational talking will take place. Family ties of this sort will create a closeness and an understanding that can happily span a lifetime, and a common affability that spreads out like the ripples on a pond.

When in love, which is not uncommon, Gemini and Libra seem to embark on a wonderful adventure. It's true that some of the practicalities of life might fall by the wayside but the gains generally outweigh the problems. Geminis take Librans by the hand and lead them through some of their own self-doubts into fresh vistas. Librans, meanwhile, being the natural diplomats of the zodiac, calm the wayward and nervous tendencies of Gemini and understand this zodiac sign well. Poetry and natural magic are possible here, which in extreme cases cause a reaction that makes it difficult for outsiders to really know where Gemini ends and Libra begins.

 ## GEMINI meets SCORPIO

Gemini can adapt itself to cope with almost any other sort of individual because it is truly the chameleon of the zodiac. For this reason, even an unlikely association such as Gemini and Scorpio is not at all out of the question. If there are any natural problems, they tend to arise from a difficulty on the part of Gemini to understand what makes Scorpio tick. Those born under the sign of the Twins have an insatiable curiosity and are inclined to look at others carefully and to pigeon-hole them as a result. Scorpio is so very complex that this process becomes awkward, if not impossible.

The motivating forces within Gemini and Scorpio are quite different. Gemini is all rush and push, whilst Scorpio takes a far more considered view of life. Both signs are capable of successes in life, but they are achieved in radically different ways. Gemini can become exasperated by Scorpio's painstaking approach, whilst the Scorpion finds Gemini too flippant and perhaps a little vulgar. However, when a bridge is achieved between two such different types, the cross-fertilisation can be useful to both. Scorpio is a deeply passionate sign and loves with every fibre of its being. Gemini people would often wish to be the same but the problem is that there are just too many people in the world and Gemini wants to understand and love them all. This is an impossible task and one that Scorpio would never attempt.

Scorpio's tendency to be jealous can present a potential stumbling-block to what might be a deep and personal relationship. Gemini is not the most constant or loyal sign and in any case it needs stimuli coming from a number of different directions. The Scorpion does not generally want to share its relationships with other individuals and can become sulky with Gemini as a result. Where such problems are overcome early, there is a good chance for lasting success, though this relationship is always going to be somewhat out of the ordinary because it represents an alliance of two people with wholly different approaches and a meeting-point that is difficult to define. All in all, this is a less than likely match – but by no means impossible.

 GEMINI meets SAGITTARIUS

Light the blue touch paper, then stand back and watch the display. Gemini and Sagittarius are opposites and yet the shows they put on for the world are very similar in many ways. Both signs are known as positives and each has a message to impart to the world – no, hundreds or thousands of messages. From the word go, this is bound to be a very reactive coming-together and it should be made plain from the outset that the real fly in the ointment relates to control. When faced with a quieter, more reflective zodiac sign, Gemini does not seem anxious to dominate, but there is something about Sagittarius that makes those born under the influence of the Twins sharpen their mental processes and prepare for action.

Sagittarius is friendly, but, like Gemini, it is an intellectual 'grazer' in the pasture of life. Its quick-thinking, no-nonsense approach is exactly matched by that of Gemini, which in any case tends to react similarly to almost every other zodiac sign. A working attachment between these two can lead to a financial wonderland – or it will, that is, if both parties have not given way to absolute exhaustion on the way. Both of these zodiac signs could sell refrigerators to Eskimos and each would want its own success to be the greatest in any given period of time.

It is difficult to imagine what sort of long-term romantic relationship can be created by those born under the Twins and the Archer. This will be a love affair par excellence, with magnificent gestures, flamboyant words, bouquets of flowers and lyrical poems. However, when the heat dies down, there has to be some sort of concrete and practical foundation to any relationship and there are occasions when this whole romance is based on shifting sand. Spats are common between individuals of these signs and they can turn, in the fullness of time, to a sort of competitive struggle that may not be pleasant either to behold or to experience.

Finding a common purpose seems to be the important factor, together with a establishing a learning process that encourages both signs to slow down somewhat. If it lasts a few months, this relationship might endure!

 ## GEMINI meets CAPRICORN

Although the inspirational qualities of Gemini are almost certain to take a back seat when the sign comes face to face with Capricorn, there is every chance that these individuals will get on very well. Capricorn is slow, methodical and sometimes even plodding. The one certainty is that it always gets where it wants to go in the end, usually by dint of perseverance. This fact is of great interest to Gemini, who is sometimes inclined to fall at the first hurdle if its plans are thwarted in some way. Working together, Capricorn can gain from Gemini a greater zest for life, more personal confidence and a friend who seems genuinely understanding. Gemini is forced to take a much deeper view of life, which slows some of its frenetic tendencies and leads it towards greater contemplation.

As friends or workmates, Gemini and Capricorn form an interesting pair. Capricorns may be steadier than Gemini, but that doesn't mean that they have no social tendencies. All they need, in order to be the most lively person in the room, is greater confidence, and this is supplied by the Gemini half of the equation. Gemini has the ability to bring out the very funny side of Capricorn, which can be extremely showy when it really feels comfortable around other people.

When the relationship between these signs eventually becomes much more than friendship, it tends to do so quite gradually. Capricorn simply will not be rushed. Geminis may not care for this fact but they had better get used to the situation if they want to stay on terms with the Goat. Family commitments will be strong here, and although there can be deep love and great happiness, it's an odds-on certainty that Gemini and Capricorn will have as many separate interests as common ones. This is probably a good thing because Gemini especially needs constant input from other people, which will be put to good use later in long talks with Capricorn. Gemini is the reporter of life, whilst the Goat is a willing reader of the mental journal that Gemini concocts. There are plenty of examples in the world to demonstrate that this pairing can work well.

 ## GEMINI meets AQUARIUS

There is much to favour this union, on almost any level. Aquarius is probably one of the oddest of the signs of the zodiac. Aquarians are inspirational, quirky, original and utterly classless. These are all qualities that are easily digested by Gemini and actually relished in the main. The two signs are 'cousins' in any case, since they both belong to the Air element. Gemini loves the unpredictability of Aquarian responses and enjoys the same tendency to do things simply on instinct. Cohesion is not really present in either sign, though both shift well enough by relying on their instincts.

When together, Gemini and Aquarius will put on a double act that positively demands an audience, and playing to the gallery comes as second nature to both parties. Aquarius may be somewhat quieter than Gemini, but certainly not much, and Aquarians will never be overshadowed by anyone. These individuals are inclined to work well together and bring a breath of fresh air and a new approach to almost anything they address. Family ties of this sort come about very frequently and usually promote a harmonious, if somewhat reactive, attachment. Gemini and Aquarius are both natural party animals and age is no criterion when assessing the magnetism that passes back and forth in this alliance.

Great scope exists here for a long and happy personal attachment. True, it will often be considered an unusual one by other people, but the very originality of the pairing is what gives it zest and potential staying-power. Expect a few tiffs, if only because Gemini and Aquarius both want to rule the roost. Such power struggles are more or less inevitable but are hardly likely to lead to any serious or long-term disagreements.

These are people who share a common desire to have fun, but who both seek to expand their knowledge of the world and its infinite diversity. The signs of Gemini and Aquarius breed people of above-average intelligence, and a relationship between them is one that exists as much in the mind as anywhere else. Advantages come through their quick thinking, travel and their potential for sharing.

GEMINI meets PISCES

Attachments and abiding friendships between Air-sign Gemini and Water-ruled Pisces are quite common. Maybe this isn't so surprising because there are needs on both sides that are generally easily addressed. Gemini seeks knowledge – its only real reason for existing at all. Pisces plumbs the world from depths that are impossible for others to reach. In its own way, each sign really only wants to know more about itself and the world at large, and both are willing to draw from resources outside their own experience.

Geminis love the high life, especially when they are young. Pisces is a more a stay-at-home type, but the combination is more balanced than either position. Even in a working situation Gemini is the one who finds compromise more difficult but it is a sign that responds well to kindness, which is exemplified by those born under the zodiac sign of the Fishes.

Pisceans are extremely emotional and Gemini offers the means by which such emotions can float closer to the surface of life. As with the Scorpio attachment, Gemini's association with Pisces can lead to some potential for jealousy, though Pisceans would handle the situation rather better. Pisceans need constant grooming of their ego if they are to be truly happy and the average Gemini is just the right individual to spend hours working with the mental hairbrush. The result can be a deep and abiding love, which is as much born of a deep respect and an enduring 'mutual appreciation society' as anything else.

Pisceans are great natural homemakers and can offer the sort of stability that Gemini individuals probably need far more than they realise. Professionally, in the family or in love, this pairing tends to work well. The natural duality of the two signs may be the only real drawback because neither zodiac sign knows itself as well as it may pretend to do. However, compromises are frequent and the shortfall in one is the talent of the other. As a result, the prognosis is good for an enduring, deep and genuinely fond attachment.

Chapter 4
Cancer
22 June to 22 July

It might seem to be a paradox that a combination such as this could possibly work but nevertheless this often proves to be the case. In Aries we find a dynamic individual, always on the go and shooting from the hip. Cancer is quieter, more contemplative and much deeper. It could be the sheer difference of the two zodiac signs that brings the possibility of success, mainly because each takes from the other those qualities that they don't possess in abundance themselves. For example, Aries lacks personal stability, which it can readily imbibe from Cancer; at the same time, the Crab shows a tendency to hesitate over decisions, which the Ram certainly does not.

Cancer is a natural homemaker and enjoys organising. The Crab deals effectively with routines, which the Ram finds difficult to address. Even in a work environment, these qualities can be important to impetuous, fiery Aries, who does need a sense of stability and a base from which to thrust its progressive qualities out into the world. Their overall attitudes to life are extremely different, though this should not prevent an eventual coming-together. What we are really looking at is an example of mutual appreciation, even when the motivating principles of life are radically different.

In times gone by, this pairing, when experienced at a personal and a romantic level, usually worked out best with a male Arian and a female Cancerian. Aries would bring home the bacon, whilst Cancer created a comfortable environment for all concerned. Now the situation is just as likely to be reversed, though in these liberated times an Aries woman and a Cancerian man would prove to be a less likely combination for all manner of reasons. The Ram automatically seems to put a protecting arm around the Crab, which is exactly what the sign of Cancer wants. It's true that this pair can't share everything – there are just too many differences – but this should not prevent a long and happy union. However, it is important that Arians always encourage their Cancerian partners to express their point of view.

CANCER meets TAURUS

When seen from the perspective of Cancer, this coming-together might look more attractive than it ultimately turns out to be. Cancer and Taurus find it difficult to fall out and there is a natural tendency for a cultured relationship, with mutual respect flowing in both directions. What really seems to be lacking here, however, is any sort of dynamism or spark. It's true that Cancer and Taurus would work very well together. In such a situation it is possible that Taurus would tend to take the lead, though co-operation is more or less inevitable.

Cancer and Taurus are both negative signs; that is, they tend to be more introvert than extrovert. Negative signs work at their best in combination with more positive types, when the opportunities for movement and activity are better. Left to their own devices, Taureans especially can be quite lazy, and easy-going Cancer may find it difficult to urge the sometimes stubborn Bull to do anything at all. In terms of romance and marriage, this may give rise to some difficulties.

The problem is that Cancer, at heart, longs for adventure. Taurus can be a real stop-at-home and the Crab may find it hard to express its own quiet, but deep-felt, desire for new experiences. There has to be a real effort here to provide the variety that brings the spice of life. Long winter evenings by the fire are very important, but so are bright lights and fun. All the same, both these zodiac signs deal well with adversity and will work long and hard to build a comfortable home and raise a family they can be proud of. Together they frequently form an association of quiet, refined pursuits, which certainly works well at a family level, where arguments and strife are not to be recommended. There may be some doubt in the mind of an outsider, who asks: 'Are you both really, genuinely happy with your lot?' But since the answer will probably turn out to be a puzzled expression on both faces, then maybe it doesn't matter that there is a lack of excitement.

 ## CANCER meets GEMINI

This tends to be a particularly well-accented relationship, and especially so from the perspective of Cancer. Most Gemini subjects are bright, full of zest and anxious to look at each and every aspect of life. Those born under the Twins have a fantastic interest in the very 'workings' of the universe, but they don't get bogged down in this, and show tremendous immediacy. This might be part of what Cancerians like about Gemini because they harbour a latent desire to see and experience everything they can. In other words,

Gemini represents a door to the world for the more reserved and often hesitant Crab.

It would appear that there is a natural magnetism here, of a kind that isn't dependent on gender, age or circumstance. In the world at large, Cancer and Gemini people are to be found working jauntily and happily, side by side. Cancer is able to bring stability to the sign of the Twins and prevents Gemini from making some of the silly mistakes that would otherwise be the case. On the reverse side of the coin, Gemini makes Cancer happy, encouraging the Crab to stretch itself and try all manner of activities that it otherwise might not consider.

In a deep and meaningful relationship, both Cancer and Gemini can be blissfully happy, though it is very important for the Cancerian half of the equation to speak its mind, for Gemini may develop a tendency to browbeat the Crab into situations that it would not normally choose. Cancer may also tend to be the sign that holds the purse strings in the relationship, simply because Gemini individuals are not very good with money.

This is a common attachment, even at a marital level, and it offers many of the hallmarks of potential success. The end result is the gradual evolution of a common purpose, together with the sort of satisfaction that doesn't exist for the sign of Cancer in some other associations. The Crab is kind, giving and sincere, factors that even capricious Gemini comes to recognise. The love, attention and genuine passion that flow back towards the Crab from Gemini are completely natural and spontaneous.

 CANCER meets CANCER

The potential success or failure of this pairing is more or less totally geared to circumstance and the sort of association that is involved. Cancer tends to be quiet and reserved, unless it is stimulated in some way by an outside influence. It stands to reason therefore that two Cancerians together are hardly likely to set the world alight. In reality, at least at the level of common friendship and even work, this probably isn't the case. Cancer may be quiet but it is also extremely sociable and can be quite chatty. Thus two Crabs will probably work well together and can prove to be good, reliable and close 'mates'. Added to this, many Cancerians have an instinctive fear of the unknown. This means that working or associating with another Crab is something akin to looking in a mirror, which can be very comfortable but is not exactly taxing.

Long-term relationships of a personal nature between two Cancerians are not all that rare. These associations don't generally provide the movers and shakers of society but they can exist comfortably in some leafy suburb, and generally enjoy a happy family life. Life may become hum-drum, though the house will always be tidy and there will certainly be food on the table. Cancerians can work hard to achieve their common objectives and will show genuine love and concern, one for the other. It is true that an outsider may feel that there is something missing – that vital spark that makes for challenge and excitement. But in a way this doesn't matter because we only miss those things that we know to exist. Cancer and Cancer when living and loving together may well have everything they need to achieve a fulfilled life.

Certainly there is a common pride in the material possessions of life, as well as a deep and abiding love for family. Friends may be a somewhat rarer commodity, but where they do exist they will also be cherished and brought into the embrace of the Cancerian household.

This relationship certainly will not be everyone's cup of tea – but then again, not everyone has to live it and as long as the parties concerned are content, everything in the garden will be rosy. A word of caution, however – some kind of outside stimulus is vital, if only to create movement and prevent the relationship from stagnating entirely.

 ## CANCER meets LEO

Everyone, whatever sign they belong to, wants to be loved – that's a universal truth. However, the Crab is more in need of direct, positive proof of affection than almost any other zodiac sign. This may be one of the reasons why the association of Cancer and Leo is a potentially favourable one on almost any level. Although reserved and sometimes difficult to understand, Cancer has great desires and aspirations. Leo is naturally in a good position to provide the circumstances under which these can be fully exploited. Leo can help Cancer at work, by encouraging enthusiasm, building confidence and offering opportunities. Since the two signs naturally get on well together, there should also be mutual contentment that oils the wheels of progress towards common objectives. Leo 'does' and Cancer makes it easy for Leo to 'do'.

Leo is bold, aspiring, frank and fearless. These are all qualities that look especially attractive to the Crab and ones that it often wishes it possessed in greater measure. Meanwhile, in Cancer the Lion sees stability, a dignified but steadfast determination and an ability to progress, even under difficult circumstances. Put the whole package together and practically every aspect of life is catered for by one side or the other. Both signs are willing to share and Leo will always listen to Cancer, just as long as the Crab is willing to speak its mind.

This can be a formidable combination when it comes to making money. Both signs are ethical and fair, both with each other and with the world at large. Family concerns are held in common, with Leo often taking the more authoritarian stance in the raising of children.

The sign of the Lion has much to offer, but it needs a secure and steady base from which to project itself into the world. This is supplied by Cancer, which itself succeeds better when under the protecting influence of the Lion. There may be shortfalls of course: for example, the very quietness of Cancer can allow the more bullying side of Leo to predominate. All in all, however, the Crab and the Lion are apt to be good, faithful and genuinely affectionate friends and partners.

 ## CANCER meets VIRGO

This is a potentially complex relationship and one that needs teasing out carefully in order to appreciate the good and bad points. Both signs are reserved, though Virgo appears less so in a day-to-day sense. Each is also given to worrying, with Virgo definitely in the lead. Cancer and Virgo both respond well to the incentives, offers and stimuli that come from an association with people who are more dynamic than themselves; both signs are also inclined to be natural home birds, who don't interact with the world as much as other zodiac signs do.

Put all these factors together and it can be appreciated that Cancer and Virgo together are hardly likely to set the world on fire. Virgo is fussy and nervy. A good, solid Cancerian friend can help to nullify these tendencies somewhat, and in any case Cancer won't offer Virgo a great deal to fuss or worry about. A quiet life suits Virgo individuals, although, being ruled by Mercury, they are more mentally motivated than they realise and do respond well to outside stimulus. Cancerians may be able to offer this, but they do require something similar themselves. Thus, even at the level of friendship, this pairing could be compared to a sports car, with nobody to turn the ignition key.

The path to success here depends on one or other of the individuals actively taking the lead. Both signs can do this, and in any case once the incentives are offered and the vehicle is rolling, life takes on its own impetus and becomes more interesting for both parties.

A romance involving Cancer and Virgo will be a quiet affair. Both signs, particularly Cancer, understand constancy and each is a natural homemaker (woe betide anyone who spills biscuit crumbs on the carpet of this household). Natural warmth is sometimes lacking from Virgo, who can be matter-of-fact and take a cold, intellectual view of life. But Cancer is the one zodiac sign that can heat up the Virgin. Despite this, when it comes to love and marriage, this probably isn't a very common relationship, mainly because these are individuals who probably would not come together in the first place. On those occasions when they do, work is needed on both sides to ensure success.

 ## CANCER meets LIBRA

The keynote of this association is harmony. Cancer and Libra have a natural understanding and tend to get on very well under virtually all circumstances. This is not to suggest that this is the best coming-together for either sign, but equally it isn't one that is apt to create problems. Librans are represented by the Scales, which of course means balance, a fact that is readily understood by Cancerians, who don't want to make waves either, despite being under a Water sign and ruled by the Moon. Gains come through their shared objectives, easy-going attitude towards others and sensible approach to life.

Even when it involves common friendship, this association more or less forces Libra into the driving seat, a position that Librans don't always relish. Nevertheless, they do tend to feel a sense of responsibility towards ever-affable Cancer, who will generally be happy to allow them to make the running. Both signs have a vested interest in giving to others; they can work well together and will rarely, if ever, argue. The deep-seated agendas of these zodiac signs may be somewhat different, but as far as the world can see, they are individuals who cheerfully commit themselves to necessary tasks. Cancer and Libra together are outgoing, co-operative and often fairly successful.

Cancer is a great dreamer, and so is Libra. At a deep level, this relationship might fail to prosper overall as a result. Perhaps there is not sufficient 'bite' here and the lack of a dynamic purpose may end up frustrating both parties on occasions. Home life will be steady and generally happy, and will look inviting when viewed from the perspective of outsiders. Both signs love to please each other and their capacity for forming deep attachments is shared. Libra is not quite as constant by nature as Cancer, and this may sometimes lead to a little friction, though on the whole we have a pairing here that can work very well both temporarily and in the long term. Family members are important and both will participate well as parents.

 ## CANCER meets SCORPIO

When two Water signs such as Cancer and Scorpio get together, the results are generally good, though with certain reservations. This is an association that tends to force Cancer on to the back foot. Scorpio is a 'negative' sign, but the average observer would sometimes fail to understand why this should be the case. If forced to take command, Scorpio can be quietly dominant, often caustic and occasionally ruthless. None of these traits is typical of Cancer and so, in almost all cases, this relationship nudges Scorpio into a position of responsibility. This does not mean that Cancer fails to contribute to the scenario. On the contrary, the very affability of the Crab is appealing to almost anyone, and Scorpio is no exception. The sting in the tail of the Scorpion will hardly ever be displayed to the Crab and life, at work, in the family or in a home environment, should be peaceful.

Again paradoxically for two of the negative signs of the zodiac, Cancer and Scorpio together are definitely inclined to travel a good deal. This broadens the horizons of both and where the relationships exists on a romantic and life-partnership level, Cancer and Scorpio can often end up living far from the shores of their birth. Anything that broadens the common experience base of the two signs tends to be fortunate and it is important for this pairing to establish, and maintain, a broad network of individual and common friends from other parts of the zodiac.

Scorpios are very aware of family members, upon whom they rely heavily. To compensate, they are very protective of those they love and this would be especially true for Cancerian individuals. A love match here would bring deep passion, and particularly so from Scorpio, with a rather more stifled demonstrative reaction from the somewhat less reactive Crab. The qualities of determination and tenacity that Scorpio derives from Mars may not show at all in this association because the average Cancerian knows very well how to keep Scorpio happy and would not deliberately upset any apple-cart.

CANCER meets SAGITTARIUS

This is one of the situations in which individuals born under the sign of Cancer can truly be swept off their feet, at least for a while. When seen from the position of the generally quiet Crab, Sagittarians can appear wonderful. People carrying the influence of the Archer are charming, lively, convincing, visibly intelligent, original and aspiring. There is much in this list that Cancer envies, for hardly anyone born under the sign of the Crab truly appreciates what they already are. We can expect some hero-worship here and that almost always means the Crab looking with adoring eyes at the Archer.

Even at the level of everyday friendship this state of affairs is unlikely to last, however. It is true that Sagittarius can make an excellent first impression, but it doesn't always fulfil this initial promise in the fullness of time. This can disappoint the Crab, especially if certain dreams and expectations have to be modified as a result. What Cancer needs to realise in this association is that Sagittarius does achieve a great deal – simply not as much as it sets out to do.

The average Archer is no cleverer than the Crab, and is inclined to get Cancer talking more than would be the case in some other zodiac matches. It is pleased to offer encouragement and genuinely wants its opposite number to prosper. The presence of Cancer 'levels out' a nature that is inclined to fly too high and offers a place of retreat for the Archer when the pressures of life become too great.

There is great activity in this relationship, sometimes too much for the Crab, but there is also a good deal of genuine excitement and a deep-seated mutual respect. There are times when Sagittarius can be somewhat overbearing but this tends to happen only when it is openly confronted, which simply isn't the Cancerian way. Money matters may be variable, simply because Sagittarius is often either very rich or very poor. The Crab is more careful and shows a frugal approach that the Archer may not like very much, but which it is certain to come to respect with the passing of time.

 CANCER meets CAPRICORN

The zodiac signs of Cancer and Capricorn are opposites, meaning that in terms of the zodiac wheel they appear six signs apart. Thus we find that Cancer is a sign of the summer, whilst Capricorn is one that appears during the winter. This tells us a good deal about the difference between Cancer and Capricorn. Just look at the contrast presented by the warm, affectionate simplicity of Cancer and the wry, sometimes caustic and more complicated qualities of Capricorn. The very difference between the two signs can bring a tendency for mutual respect and set the stage for a good association.

Capricorn may well be the most practical sign of them all. Goats work hard to achieve their objectives and are willing to please. They have basically logical and tidy minds and do not rely on intuition in the way that Cancerians do. Capricorn wants material success in life, but it knows that this won't be achieved overnight. The Crab may be less sure about the potential for happiness brought about by mere wealth and possessions but is probably more than willing to go along for the ride. These two signs, though opposites, are unlikely to fall out. Both are also what are known as 'cardinal' signs, which makes them astrological cousins, and whilst the combination of Water and Earth that lies at the heart of this alliance can prove a little stultifying on occasions, it is rarely potentially difficult.

If there is a problem here it may stem from the fact that although things get done, the level of excitement that the Crab wants, at least subconsciously, may not be present. Neither of these individuals is inclined to take chances and the desire for travel, latent in the Crab, may be suppressed by the more stay-at-home Capricorn.

Both these people are family types and Cancer particularly so, but at the deepest level this may be a commitment without a great deal of passion. Whether that pleases Cancer at the end of the day, or after a few years, must remain to be seen. Someone needs to ring the changes on a regular basis when this association exists at a personal level and a good deal of the effort in this regard does need to come from the direction of the Goat.

 ## CANCER meets AQUARIUS

Cancer is one of the most pleasant and kind of all the zodiac signs. Since many people believe this to be also true of Aquarius, there is plenty of scope for a fortunate coming-together in this case. Crabs are generally quiet, but are always ready for a laugh, and they will enjoy many smiles in their association with the Water Bearer. Aquarius has a very 'off-the-wall' approach to life and one that sometimes perplexes Cancer. It is far more dynamic and more inclined to take chances, which occasionally horrifies but also fascinates the Crab. With the passing of time, Cancerians learn to stretch themselves to accommodate the needs of Aquarius, a sign they generally respect. This is good for both parties, even in a casual friendship or in a working association.

Aquarius has great aspirations and a strong social conscience but it is naturally far more selfish than Cancer because its motivations are nearly always geared towards its own requirements. Cancer can teach Aquarius to steer its many powers towards helping others in the world at large, which makes the Water Bearer also feel more fulfilled.

In business, this can be a powerful combination. Aquarius has the ability to bring out the very best in Cancer under almost all circumstances and there is good potential here for making money. Their working environment is likely to be reactive, sparky and generally happy.

Aquarians make good lovers – at least for as long as they are interested. Cancer has ways and means to keep that interest flowing. Aquarius lacks stability, which the Crab can bring to almost any situation. Boredom is not likely and the prognosis for a happy relationship is good. Whether or not these two individuals ever actually come to understand each other fully remains to be seen, however. They are motivated by different qualities. Cancer works from an emotional base, Aquarius from a more intellectual one. At best this makes for a complementary situation that works well, but occasionally this lack of common incentive needs to be resolved.

CANCER meets PISCES

Cancer and Pisces will hardly ever find any reason to fall out with each other. How could they? Both are motivated by the same basic desires and each is an extremely emotional zodiac sign. They share compassion, a deep social conscience and a desire to nurture. Neither sign is particularly gritty or reactive. All of this contributes to a good potential for friendship, and for working towards common objectives in a family sense. Both signs can rise slowly and steadily to positions of some authority and each would respect the position and thought processes of the other.

This is a pairing that probably works better at a superficial friendship or family level than it does romantically. Problems arise when the two signs form a lifelong pact, which can so easily happen between people who seem to have so much in common. Cancer and Pisces both work at their best when there is something to push against, but each is a Water sign, and we all know what happens when we try to push water – it simply recedes. Life for these two will be fairly easy-going, with a lack of disruption and arguments and a sense of common purpose. What may be lacking is the sort of excitement that makes both these zodiac signs feel more fulfilled. Either may take the lead under different circumstances but neither is not keen on taking chances, and as a result life can sometimes appear to be quite tedious. Much energy will be put into the home and family, however. A comfortable atmosphere is necessary for both the Crab and the sign of the Fishes and this is not difficult for the combination to achieve.

Cancer and Pisces can seem to be blissfully happy. Only if the observer plumbs the subconscious depths of this pairing may they come to realise that things are not quite as simple as they first appear. Attention needs to be given to pushing back the boundaries of a world that can become just too comfortable when Cancer and Pisces are together. Deliberately setting new horizons will offer incentives that both these signs need at heart.

Chapter 5
Leo

23 July to 23 August

 LEO meets ARIES

The potential problem with this pairing stems from the fact that each of these signs is dynamic, aspiring, forceful and determined and neither is anxious to play second fiddle to anyone. It's true that there is almost certain to be a grudging respect here, even if the more generous-spirited and noble Leo doesn't always approve of the methods Aries uses to get on in life. Things work better when the Ram involved is willing to admit that they can't do everything. At least that way the Lion will get a look in too and then a more positive union may develop.

In any work situation, Leo and Aries both need to be at the top of the tree and there isn't always room for that. As natural leaders, both signs prefer to reign supreme and whilst Leo will willingly defer to a less dynamic sign out of choice, it will rarely do so if any element of force is exerted. Family relationships can be somewhat turbulent when the Lion and the Ram are involved, and spats of one sort of another are more than likely. Some level of understanding does exist between them, however, because both these zodiac signs are Fire signs and so Leo and Aries can at least become good friends.

From a personal and romantic point of view, this is an 'all or nothing' sort of union. Leo and Aries will either enjoy the love affair of the century, or drive each other mad very quickly indeed. When genuine mutual reliance is established, this is a formidable combination and one that could lead to masses of common aims and objectives. All too frequently, however, a sort of competition will arise on a daily or even an hourly basis. Lines of demarcation need to be established early, giving each partner in this relationship responsibility over specific areas of life. Co-operation at every level would be better but this may prove to be an unattainable goal.

This isn't the worst union by any means, but it is certainly going to take effort on both sides if it is going to prosper in the longer term.

LEO meets TAURUS

The general tenor of this association is positive for both zodiac signs. Taurus tends to like and respect Leo almost instinctively, whilst the Lion is easily swayed by such respect and in any case can readily develop a fondness for the Bull. Leo, strangely, will do almost anything for anyone – provided that no pressure is put upon it. Taurus doesn't try to alter the Lion's attitude or proclivities and thus finds itself almost always on the winning side of Leo's generous ways.

The average Taurean is certainly very much quieter than a Leo subject will usually be and tends to be happy to have things that way, but a Bull is not a pushover – they are powerful people in their own right. Leo usually recognises this fact and is wise enough not to try to take advantage.

As friends, Leo and Taurus can endure for a lifetime. The very great mutual respect that develops quite early in this association is apt to continue unabated. There should be few rows, mainly because despite the fact that Taurus is a 'fixed' sign, and so apt to be rigid, Leo is 'mutable', or flexible, so that they are unlikely to find themselves at loggerheads. In any work situation the signs are complementary. Leo may adopt a more public persona than Taurus, who is happier as a rule when working behind the scenes. This is not always the case, but generally speaking Taurus takes a supporting role, whilst Leo is the active partner.

A coming-together of a more personal or domestic sort may raise a few problems, particularly since Taurus usually likes to rule the roost, a fact that could just be resented by Leo on occasions. All in all, however, there is enough difference between these zodiac signs to allow for individuality to flourish alongside co-operation. The household will be lively and entertaining and even the Bull's legendary stubborn ways are less evident when the Lion is prepared to be flexible, leaving Taurus nothing to push against.

This can be a happy association at any level and could also turn out to be profitable. Leo and Taurus are both good workers and Taurus squirrels money away readily. The pairing exists on a practical as well as an intellectual level and rarely lacks interest.

 # LEO meets GEMINI

This is a very promising relationship, full of action, reaction and energy. Leo is proud, bold, generous of spirit and very regal. Gemini meanwhile is the jackdaw of the zodiac, picking up attractive pieces of information wherever it goes and storing them away for later use. Twins are charming, full of compliments and perfectly suited to approaching the Leo throne with just the right honeyed words to get what they want from the Lion. It isn't a one-way street, however. Leo gains from having a ready mouthpiece and is generally fed a number of interesting ideas from Gemini, who never stops looking for the next angle.

As friends, Leo and Gemini should be very good to be around. You are unlikely to find this pair skulking together at the back of the library or locked into some mutual pursuit that requires isolation. Rather, Leo and Gemini are out there in the larger world, usually associating with groups of people and ready to join in the cut and thrust of everyday life. This is probably similar to what happens when the Lion and the Twins come together in a family setting. At gatherings of all kinds, these individuals tend to gravitate towards each other and they are the sort of people who will put on the best show.

Leos and Geminis also work well together, with the Lion usually being responsible for the decision-making and the Twins implementing ideas and taking the lead where associations with the world at large are concerned.

Leo and Gemini can form happy social attachments with each other but are also well suited in long-term or marital relationships. Together they will create a happy and generally carefree environment – the sort of home that others will want to visit. Both are sociable, so there ought to be plenty of shindigs, dinner parties and the like. Jealousy between the two is probably kept to a minimum but Gemini does tend to be something of a wanderer, something that the average Leo won't respond to positively.

When these two come together sparks fly – but they represent the sort of firework display that everyone wants to see. Leo and Gemini generally care deeply for each other, and at the end of the day that's what matters.

 ## LEO meets CANCER

When Leo and Cancer get together, the most important feature is the great interdependence that arises from the relationship. These are truly complementary zodiac signs; each one possesses what the other lacks. Leo is ambitious, positive, go-ahead and brave. Cancer is retiring, but extremely sensitive, intuitive and deep. In any sort of relationship, it is able to support Leo by offering advice and by causing the Lion to look deeper into its own motivations. The Lion works best when it has a purpose and although the Crab is not the most active sign in the zodiac it has plenty of ideas, which Leo is pleased to put into practice. Cancer, in turn, responds to a protecting arm and that's exactly what the Lion has to offer.

It takes all types of people to make the world go round, a fact that is readily understood by both Leo and Cancer. As a result their relationship enjoys flexibility, understanding and a deep, abiding mutual respect. This makes any sort of association that much easier and ensures that neither does anything without consultation and verification. True, the two individuals may often think about certain aspects of life in radically different ways, but that does not mean that that conflict is apt to arise. In many cases the Lion and the Crab simply won't ever come to disagreeing in any real sense. Cancer is deep, however, and this may give rise to problems. Lions are much more immediate in their approach to life than their retiring Crab partners.

These two possess the ability to build a happy home together. It is an especially fortunate combination for the raising of children, who will receive a balanced and interesting start to life. Leo, when on its own, is not specifically a homemaker, so ideas about décor, furnishings and domestic details tend to be left to the Crab, who is more than willing to take such considerations on board. The Lion and the Crab can be deep and ardent lovers, but first and foremost they are likely to be very good friends. This may well be the most important factor.

 ## LEO meets LEO

When two Leos come together, the outcome is often decided by the first encounter. One of the reasons that this is likely to be a successful association is that Leo is a zodiac sign that, at heart, likes itself. And when you see a reflection of your own personality coming at you from the direction of another person, it helps if at least a little self-love is present. True, Leo is a dominant Fire sign, but it responds more positively to the reactions it gets from others than does its brother sign, Aries. Since most Leos are proud, bold, protective and caring, two Leos together should display these virtues to an even greater extent.

In the workplace, a brace of Lions can prove to be formidable. They may not naturally gravitate towards each other when in a group setting, but once such an alliance is formed, it will soon become deep, effective and mutually generous. Such a situation could mark the beginning of a friendship, and one that could easily endure for some time. Leos want to be liked, but at the same time they need to control, so don't expect an association totally free from disagreements. It is just as well therefore that the Lion is not really inclined to bear a grudge and displays a temper that may be formidable, but is not long-lasting.

When deciding upon a life together, two Leo individuals have to realise from the outset that there can be no leader and no follower. Responsibilities have to be shared equally and then followed rigidly. For example, two Leos attempting to co-operate in cooking the same meal are certain to trip each other up at every turn. It would be far better to take the chores in turn and to do them individually.

There is certainly passion here, together with common interests that will take the pair out into the big, wide world beyond the front door. However, Leos, like the lion itself, can be very lazy on occasions. It is going to take a good deal of interdependent motivation to create the very real material success that both desire.

 ## LEO meets VIRGO

If a situation requires determination, practical application and dynamism, then look no further than the alliance of Leo and Virgo. From the outset, however, this is not always going to be an easy match. Leo is a 'fixed' sign, and Virgo often seems to exemplify a 'fixed' attitude, because of its Earth-sign ruling. Many zodiac signs have the ability to bring out the best in the Lion, but Virgo is probably not one of them. Leo rarely bothers to think, preferring to go straight into action – this is the reason why so many soldiers born under this zodiac sign have won medals for gallantry. As a rule, this is a fine attribute, but it doesn't necessarily go down well with Virgo, who is more careful, considered and quite fussy.

The saving grace in the relationship may be conversation. Although possessing a sort of hidden, natural reserve, Virgos like to talk and can manage to achieve a rapport with Leos. Once the individuals concerned really begin to know each other, a common respect will begin to develop. Leo needs to flex its muscles out there in the real world, and Virgo respects the forthright, magnanimous qualities of the Lion, because it has leanings in this direction itself. Even in a friendship situation, Virgo can often supply the means to put Leo plans into action, or at the very least to finish and round them off. The mental motivation of the Virgin is really quite different to that of the Lion, however, so there may always be a basic lack of understanding.

This is not a common match in marriage, perhaps because Leos and Virgos don't mix all that freely in the first place. Where it does happen, the prognosis is not bad, just as long as each is prepared to make basic alterations to their nature, and realises that they have to accommodate the other person. Virgo will do the housework, whilst probably grumbling about the fact a good deal of the time, and Leo is likely to find Virgo's naturally tidy ways frustrating. There are good intellectual connections here but Virgo can seem cold when viewed by sunny Leo.

LEO meets LIBRA

Stand by for a generally jolly time when these two meet. Libra is a zodiac sign that can get on with just about anyone and Leo presents little difficulty to those born under the Scales. There is plenty to keep both parties interested and that is what really helps to sustain this relationship. Leos and Librans both have a great interest in life and sunny Leo is stimulated greatly by the intelligence of Libra. Leo also responds well to the more refined qualities that it encounters in this meeting and does not have to make too many compromises in its own nature to accommodate Libra's winning ways. This is likely to be an ideal friendship – not one that is likely to be deeply intellectual or heavy, but a relationship based on a happy and breezy understanding.

Leo is more materialistic than Libra, but then those born under the Scales probably represent the most flexible individuals of all – that is one of the main reasons why this association is likely to work well. Leo's bold, aspiring ways will impress Libra and offer incentives that Librans do not possess when left to their own devices. Libra, on the other hand, is more intuitive than Leo, who can benefit by listening to the words of wisdom that flow forth. This is especially true in a work situation, where a feeling of mutual success and a happy workplace will result from this alliance.

This pairing provides a frequent and often very happy romantic combination. With everything to play for in the excitement stakes, Leo will be able to blow away some of the natural Libran reserve, if only because Librans so willingly adapt to others. Librans respect the protecting ways of Leo, even if they may occasionally feel somewhat stifled. This is not an association of the narrow-visioned, stay-at-home variety and there is always going to be more than enough fun to go around. This couple will have very many good friends and should be popular in almost any sort of neighbourhood. Further benefits come through mutual financial acumen and via their ability to make ground socially.

It must be said, however, that in order to achieve absolute happiness Libra needs to be less fickle and Leo less dominant.

 ## LEO meets SCORPIO

When Leo meets Scorpio, there is likely to be a struggle as these two radically different people try to get to know each other well. Scorpio is inclined to be deep, difficult to understand, sometimes sarcastic and invariably secretive. All of these qualities contrast markedly to those of Leo. It is true of course that people of opposite views can often hit it off extremely well. However, in the case of Leo and Scorpio there is the added difficulty that the individuals concerned simply may not care for each other very much – even when they do grow more familiar. Scorpions are inclined to find Leos somehow too garish, too full of majesty and altogether too grand for their own good. In return, Leo often sees Scorpio as being dark and small, with limited vision and a caustic tongue. Of course, neither picture is entirely true. The real problem is that Leo and Scorpio are both 'fixed' signs, so when they've made up their minds, nothing is going to change it.

Assuming that these individuals are forced together, through work or family attachments, what do they have in common? Well, they are both capable of speaking their minds, each is actually very kind at heart and neither will suffer fools gladly. Leo and Scorpio can both be extremely stubborn when they wish and each is capable of great success. Whether or not any of these similarities are useful in forming an alliance seems doubtful, however. What is more certain is the fact that if Leo and Scorpio ever do get together willingly they can make a formidable team.

This is a relationship that is seen only rarely on a strictly personal level. It generally works well only when one of the zodiac signs is not absolutely typical of its type. Leo and Scorpio, as archetypes, simply could not live together happily for any length of time. But if Leo learns not to take Scorpio seriously, and if the Scorpion can come to respect the bright and somewhat ostentatious qualities of the Lion, there is a chance of domestic harmony. Certainly both these zodiac signs make extremely good parents and both can commit themselves willingly to family life. But this alone is probably not enough to sustain a long-term relationship.

LEO meets SAGITTARIUS

Leo and Sagittarius can be great friends, or they may prove to be deeply at odds with each other. The blessing, which is occasionally also the curse, is the fact that both are born under Fire signs. This can prove to be great for common dynamism and even practical success but it does mean that in any sort of relationship both individuals want to be the one to rule the roost, which of course simply isn't possible. Any flexibility here is more likely to come from the direction of the Sagittarian partner, who will be naturally more adaptable than Leo.

When seen from the perspective of the Lion, Sagittarius can appear to be very interesting, especially at first. The Archer fascinates the basically slower-paced Leo – hardly surprisingly, because Sagittarius is perhaps the quickest thinker and actor of all the signs. This should be the basis for a good working relationship, though it is always going to be a reactive one and each party needs to stick strictly to what it knows.

Leo and Sagittarius can form a formidable friendship, perhaps partly because being friends means they will necessarily spend some time apart. It is only really when the two are forced together 24 hours a day that the basic differences – or, perhaps more likely, the similarities – are apt to surface and this is likely to prove the case in personal attachments. If Leo wants to paint the house red and Sagittarius doesn't, the whole thing can become much more of an issue than is necessary, involving a matter of principle that neither will concede. Only if both parties can learn to swallow a little of that Fire-sign pride will there be peace and harmony for any protracted period of time.

Leo loves deeply, whilst Sagittarius wants to do so. Archers are certainly less constant in this regard than Lions, who can become distinctly jealous when Sagittarians decide to do their own thing – as they frequently do. The pairing generally makes for a good physical relationship, however, and at those times when Sagittarius exhausts itself, Leo takes over and offers great support. The saving grace in this relationship may lie in the fact that Sagittarius can make Leo less pompous, and at the same time may itself learn patience.

 ## LEO meets CAPRICORN

The very best associations are formed when people of different proclivities come together, preserving the strengths of their own nature, whilst accommodating and even relishing those of others. This is certainly possible when Leo meets Capricorn. The Goat doesn't usually worry about being in charge – or at least it doesn't make an issue of the fact. Capricorn is also inclined to be very much more practical than Leo, and is even capable of making some of Leo's more grandiose schemes come to fruition. Capricorn is a slow and steady builder, it isn't showy or pretentious, as Leo sometimes tends to be, and yet its capabilities complement those of the Lion well. Leo is proud and even joyful, both characteristics that Capricorn needs and which it can absorb from any sort of relationship with the Lion.

One of the very best aspects of this pairing shows itself in a working relationship. Leo has great vision and tremendous strength; Capricorn is inclined to support these natural traits, offering what is known in astrology as the 'Saturn anchor'. All the grandiose schemes in the world are only of any use if there is someone on board who can deal with the 'nuts and bolts' of life, and this is what Capricorn does extremely well.

In friendship, Leo and Capricorn enjoy their differences and even revel in them. It's a peculiar sort of alliance at times but nevertheless it does tend to work.

When united by the bonds of marriage, or in fact in any form of protracted personal relationship, Leo and Capricorn can fare extremely well. Both know what is expected of them and there isn't much of a sense of competition, since neither wants to excel in the other's province. Lines of demarcation are set almost automatically and neither sign particularly desires to change the other. Despite this, this is a dynamic relationship that enjoys a common sense of purpose that might be envied by many others. This association tends to be steadfast, with great loyalty shown by both parties and very little tendency for either to create issues or arguments.

 ## LEO meets AQUARIUS

Leo people are popular, and with good cause. It's hard to fall out with someone with Leo's good qualities, and even though Lions can sometimes appear to be a little too regal, they are good-hearted, principled and genuine. These are all characteristics that tend to be particularly relished by Aquarius. Leo and Aquarius really don't approach life from at all the same standpoint, admittedly, but this need not mean that the two signs will fail to get along. On the contrary, they could turn out to be extremely good friends. Since Aquarius loves a chat, and Leo isn't exactly quiet by nature, it is likely that conversation is what brings these two together in the first place.

Aquarians are interested in anything and everything. This inquiring tendency is attractive to Leos, who for different reasons also want to get to the bottom of many situations. It doesn't really matter that the incentives are different – it's the common purpose that counts here.

Leo is an ardent and sincere friend. In this respect, there is an obvious difference, for Aquarius forms many associations and few of them are as important in the long term as those that Leo enjoys. Aquarius positively needs variety, whilst Leo, for all its showy ways, is invariably inclined to establish routines. Because both signs are flexible, at least to some degree, the result of this pairing generally achieves a sensible compromise.

Leo and Aquarius can easily fall in love, and under the right circumstances will retain a long-term mutual attachment. Leos need to be mindful of the Aquarian desire for basic freedom, though this is hardly likely to be much of a problem to Lions, who themselves refuse to be fettered. The beauty of this attachment probably lies in the fact that neither individual is likely to feel stifled and each will respect the right of the other to be different. Both signs are potentially good travellers and enjoy looking at cultures other than their own. Both strive for success and are willing to share the profit when they have put in the necessary effort. Co-operation is present in this relationship, and Leo teaches Aquarius the true value of constancy.

LEO meets PISCES

Experience shows that there is often a good deal of mileage in relationships established between Fire signs, such as Leo, and Water signs, of which Pisces is an example. However, no matter what sort of association this is, it is not likely to be a coming-together of equals. Leo and Pisces think and act in radically different ways and they rarely share a common motivation. Does this mean that the communion is going to be awkward? Not at all. The fact is that Pisces loves to be cherished, and caring for someone else comes as second nature to Leo, who will instinctively throw a protective arm around most individuals. This might be a problem to some, but not to those born under the sign of the Fishes. On the contrary, it makes Pisces feel more comfortable and brings from it the cherishing and nurturing qualities that it also naturally possesses.

At work, Leo will most likely be the one in charge – indeed the situation would be rather odd or strained if it were the other way round. Leos encourage Pisceans to talk freely and to express themselves at a more direct level. The natural warmth of the Lion can create a really comfortable atmosphere within which Pisces learns to function. This same general psychological pairing would also exist at a family level, often even if the Leo is the younger family member. As a rule, Pisceans are both ageless and classless, attributes that they naturally encourage Leo to take on board.

When it comes to a deep and meaningful relationship, there is every reason to believe that this combination is a good one all round. The only time that things may go wrong is when some sort of 'role reversal' is forced on to Leo and Pisces, but as long as the Lion feels it is in charge (whether or not this is actually the case) all should be well. Leo is loyal, and under the right circumstances so is Pisces. There may be some interests that are not – and do not have to be – held in common. For example, those born under the Fishes may not be so inclined to burn the candle at both ends as the Lion. But there is great trust in this combination, which is altogether a fortunate scenario.

Chapter 6
Virgo
24 August to 23 September

 VIRGO meets ARIES

Both partners may bring great practical aptitude to bear in this relationship. Virgoans and Arians like to get things done, even if they approach the situation from very different points of view. Aries is inclined to bulldoze its way to the top, whereas Virgo will use guile, cunning and direct argument. Virgo has the capacity to wear anyone down with words, even the irrepressible Aries. Thus, even though it is clear that the dominance here comes from the Ram, those born under the sign of the Virgin can often prove to be the winners in the end.

Virgo may find Aries overbearing and sometimes rash – and both these accusations may be true – but unfortunately Virgo frequently brings out the worst in the Ram and fails to see the good side of this extremely successful and forthright individual. Aries generally thinks that Virgo nags, whilst Virgo considers Aries to be a shallow thinker, distinctly lacking in subtlety.

It's inevitable that sometimes circumstances will force these individuals together. In a work situation, or one that occurs through family ties, there is no real choice in the matter, though it isn't likely that Aries and Virgo will become bosom buddies. But if they manage to shelve their basic differences, these signs have a great ability to complement each other and can achieve significant success by pooling their resources. Virgo brings strength, perseverance and generally good communication skills, whilst Aries adds zest and a progressive ability to bring home the bacon.

On those rare occasions when Virgo and Aries sign up for a lifetime together, it will usually be discovered that one or other of them is not really typical of their zodiac sign. If some sort of understanding can be achieved, however it comes about, there is great mileage even in this unlikely match. Mutual success in material matters is one area that can easily be cultivated, together with an agreement to be together and yet, under certain circumstances, remain apart.

VIRGO meets TAURUS

There is a meeting-point here, for both Virgo and Taurus are Earth signs. This means that both can be immensely practical and tend to take a no-nonsense view of life. In a working relationship, or if the individuals are born into the same family, this should prove to be very useful. There are situations that are distinctly helped when both parties have a common approach, though perhaps unfortunately the situation is not usually all that simple. For example, another quality shared by Taurus and Virgo is that they are both extremely stubborn. Virgo may be slightly more flexible in some situations but in any sort of association, if these individuals choose to dig their heels in, difficulties are apt to arise.

If the Virgin and the Bull hold common objectives, this can lead to great rewards, usually through great perseverance and occasionally through a deep respect for each other. For example, if these individuals come together to start a new company, they may well achieve a good deal of success. Problems only really arise when the business association develops into something much more. True, Virgo and Taurus have a great regard for each other, and there is even a sort of magnetism between them on occasions, but the relationship really works best when other people and values are added to the mix.

Taureans and Virgoans are not usually found together in the midst of domestic harmony. When it does happen, it's generally because Virgo has learned to adopt a much more flexible attitude to life with Taurus than it would allow when placed alongside another zodiac sign. Where an irresistible force meets an immovable object, something has to give, and in this case it is usually Virgo.

Both signs are kind at heart but each can be somewhat caustic and sarcastic when things are not going well. There is a need for a great deal of giving on both sides if this is going to go down as the relationship of the century. Diversions are also needed, and maybe an unconventional approach. The arrival of children will probably be a positive benefit.

 ## VIRGO meets GEMINI

Who can judge the true potential when two Mercury-ruled signs such as these come together? Virgo is often quite impressed by silver-tongued Gemini, for a while at least, and it is true that when the chips are down both these individuals have the ability to talk themselves out of trouble. Lack of communication is not, therefore, going to be a problem in any sort of association between Virgo and Gemini – in fact the exact reverse will probably tend to be the case. Gemini also has a great ability to help Virgo, because the average Virgoan will recognise in the sign of the Twins someone who can use Mercurial traits in a positive and successful manner. Meanwhile, Virgo can add some of the practicality necessary to back up Gemini's promise.

In any business association where Gemini does the selling and Virgo the organising, these signs can work together extremely successfully, though the situation will not work half as well if the roles are reversed. Virgo can become very frustrated by Gemini's lax ways – probably with some justification – although the lighter side of Virgo should also learn to laugh at such matters and simply enjoy Gemini's winning nature. Where there is shared laughter, rather than stern words, Virgo and Gemini will discover that they do have things in common and can go on to become good friends.

It is doubtful whether a Virgo–Gemini household would prove to be happy for both parties. Virgo is extremely tidy, whilst Gemini definitely is not. Those born under the sign of the Virgin adopt routines, which Gemini would find difficult, if not impossible, to address. Gemini often achieves a degree of success through gut feelings that are somewhat alien to Virgo, who may be irritated beyond belief by this. Yet when both parties realise that they are working towards a common objective and that the relationship is not some sort of competition, the happiness that can spring from this pairing is enlivening and wonderful to behold. All it takes is a little understanding on both sides, and a good utilisation of each other's best qualities.

 ## VIRGO meets CANCER

This is by no means an impossible association, even if it is quite rare. This is because Virgo and Cancer probably wouldn't become acquainted in the first place, unless the situation were forced on them. Both signs are 'negative', which inclines to an introverted tendency, though this is less so in the case of Virgo. The Crab is a deep creature, difficult to get to know and emotional to a point that Virgo might find hard to understand. Virgo does need a sense of security, however, and that's something that Cancer can offer with very little difficulty. Virgo, in turn, is likely to be of the chatty sort – there are many such Virgoans in the world – and so may be able to bring the Crab out of its shell.

This is not likely to be an argumentative association on any level. Cancer is easy-going, kind and quite unwilling to upset others unless it is absolutely forced. It can endure far more of a buffeting than it would ever get from Virgo, who is, at heart, a very kind zodiac type. These two can be mutually supportive in a career situation, or when allied by family ties, though even here the depth of understanding that each can establish with individuals elsewhere in the zodiac is apt to be missing.

When Virgo and Cancer choose to set out on a long-term, personal attachment, perhaps setting up home together, they are likely to create one of the most tidy homes to be found anywhere. What is more, both these individuals will find such surroundings very comfortable – though whether the rest of the world would agree is a different matter entirely. Virgo with Cancer is steady, secure and probably quite steadfast, which may make this relationship dangerously close to tedium. Certainly, any real interest that comes to the match will probably come from outside because, as a couple, Virgo and Cancer really require other, more dynamic, types around. When there are many common friendships there is more to talk about, and talking brings happiness to this pair. Long, quiet interludes are definitely to be avoided at all costs.

Commitment to family members, and especially to children, is definitely not in doubt.

If there is any sort of problem in this pairing, it arises because both Virgo and

 ## VIRGO meets LEO

Leo know very well what they want from life – and it isn't always exactly the same thing. Routine plays an important part in the life of Virgo, as it does for any Earth-sign individual. Leos, on the other hand, are more inclined to follow their instincts, despite being under a 'fixed', naturally inflexible zodiac sign. If both are prepared to recognise that slight alterations to their nature are required, this will make things run more smoothly.

Virgo is communicative and easy-going when relaxed and there isn't much about the outgoing, cheerful Lion that will cause friction. Where the two signs come together in a work situation, there is enough practicality here to ensure that the job gets done, and the two signs in question also have what it takes to co-operate and to enjoy themselves at the same time.

It is sometimes difficult for Leo to understand fully what motivates Virgo, for people born under this sign are not easy to assess. Furthermore, it isn't Leo's way to deal much in psychology. The best pairings of this sort occur when Virgo individuals are willing to share their thoughts, dreams and aspirations willingly, bringing them into the realm of the Lion. In this case, Leos will work hard to support and encourage their Virgo partners, who aren't half as confident as they pretend to be. It may sometimes seem to the Virgoans that the effort they have to make is disproportionate, but the results will almost certainly make the effort well worthwhile.

Virgo with Leo is not a combination that crops up very regularly in terms of life partners. This has little or nothing to do with an inability of the signs in question to get on well together – it's more because they rarely choose each other in the first place. Where they do, however, there is every reason to believe that the prognosis will be good. The relationship provides a balance between quietness and activity, plus plenty of potential success on a practical level. Virgo is naturally careful as a rule and wants a settled and happy home. These are needs that can be understood and positively addressed by Leo.

 ## VIRGO meets VIRGO

When two of the same zodiac signs meet, there are only usually two results – total triumph or total disaster. In the case of Virgo, it generally leads to the former because Virgo people almost always like and respect others of their type. What Virgoans require most is understanding but people sometimes fail to recognise just how complicated and deep they are. This is no problem when two Virgoans come together because there is a rapport here that those born under the Virgin cannot find through any other association. The more fussy and nervy qualities of Virgo are far less likely to predominate when an individual born of this sign knows that it is understood. In the end, each part of the relationship then begins to smile at its own peculiarities and deals with them in a much more light-hearted way.

As workmates, Virgo individuals don't have to second-guess each other. Since they both approach life and situations in more or less the same way, they can work together as one. Virgo is ruled by Mercury and it can be quite a talkative zodiac sign – so it is not hard to imagine what this means when two such people get together. Family ties of this sort also tend to be extremely strong, no matter what the relationship. Common objectives are easy to establish and the more entrenched type of attitude displayed by some Virgoans is much less likely to show itself under these circumstances.

The all-Virgoan type of personal relationship certainly will not be everyone's cup of tea, though it suits the parties concerned down to the ground. The double Virgoan household will be neat and tidy, though certainly not a quiet or an uneventful place. This couple tend to have friends in common and they will demonstrate a deep and abiding love that is obvious to any observer. Virgo and Virgo are almost always happy together, and the fact shines out in their dealings with the world at large. This could turn out to be one of the best zodiac pairings of them all, even if it occasionally looks somewhat odd when viewed by outsiders who come from radically different parts of the zodiac.

VIRGO meets LIBRA

There are great potential gains here, arising from the characteristics of both the zodiac signs involved. The flexibility of Libra tends to compensate for the more fixed attitude of Virgo, and since Librans are so easy to get along with, Virgo is apt to be less fussy in this association. This pairing, of any type, tends to mean there is a generally easy-going attitude with plenty of talk and many laughs. The presence of Libra is inclined to make Virgoans take themselves less seriously and promotes an open, competitive and yet relaxed atmosphere in which both zodiac signs can function well.

Arguments between these individuals, whatever the relationship, will normally be few and far between. Most Librans are such affable characters that they bring out the most protective and compliant qualities of Virgo, at the same time allowing the sign of the Virgin to function to its best capacities. In a work setting, the level of co-operation will be marked and the organisational skills of Virgo sit well with the less disciplined but more entertaining qualities of the Scales. Friendships of this sort are relaxed, and common interests develop quickly and can be maintained over a long period of time.

When Virgo and Libra come together in deeper, more personal attachments, the prognosis tends to be very good. There is likely to be great happiness here, not only for the parties themselves but also extending out into the world at large, because Virgo and Libra together spread their happiness around. If there are any drawbacks at all they may come as a result of Virgo's insistence on an ordered way of life, which doesn't come easily to Libra. Virgo should therefore avoid imposing too many rules and regulations, and instead try to enjoy and learn from the Libran capacity to derive as much pleasure as possible from every moment and situation. Family ties within the union are fairly strong and the level of liberality that comes from the sign of the Scales tends to be infectious. In this pairing, Virgo is usually much more relaxed.

 ## VIRGO meets SCORPIO

Although both these zodiac signs tend to be quite deep by nature, there is no reason why they should fail to get along reasonably well. True, this pairing isn't likely to be especially exciting when viewed by outsiders, but it's what the individuals themselves feel that really counts. Virgo understands the 'fixed' nature of the Scorpio personality and copes with it very well, even if there are going to be a few quite deep-seated disagreements and a little sulking from time to time. Virgo is quite a talkative type and tends to dominate the conversation in this relationship, though this doesn't mean that Scorpio will remain silent perpetually. The very presence of a Mercury-ruled zodiac sign such as Virgo will help Scorpio to put forward its own point of view on a fairly regular basis.

Where work is concerned, acting as partners, Virgo and Scorpio usually get a great deal done. Despite being known as a 'mutable' or 'common' sign, which implies great flexibility, Virgo remains one of the most determined zodiac signs of them all. Add this to the persistence and perseverance inherent in the Scorpion and the result can be quite formidable. This will also prove to be the case in family ties, and Virgo and Scorpio make loyal and steadfast friends, who may well maintain their relationship over many years.

A deep and abiding love can develop between Virgo and Scorpio. This may not be evident to the world at large because the individuals concerned, when together, are not likely to be over-demonstrative. Despite this, they possess a sense of common purpose and can soon establish a comfortable and even fairly luxurious home. They are likely to want to raise a family, though care needs to be taken here that children are not stifled by their naturally protective qualities.

All things considered, Virgo and Scorpio are very good for each other. With the passing of time Virgo becomes less nervy and Scorpio more communicative. In the final analysis this could be one of the best associations of all for Virgo.

 ## VIRGO meets SAGITTARIUS

In some ways it may appear at first that this relationship won't work very well at all, and yet nothing could be further from the truth. By rights, Virgo should find Sagittarians brash, less than reliable and far too showy for their own good. This doesn't happen, however, probably because Virgo recognises in the Archer certain latent traits in its own make-up that it would like to bring to the fore. Sagittarius is funny, and Virgoans are attracted to the immediacy with which Archers live their lives. Some of the natural pomposity of Virgo is side-stepped or even lampooned by Sagittarius, who can probably get away with teasing Virgo more successfully than any other zodiac sign. Virgo cannot avoid laughing at the antics and comments of the Archer.

When these two come together in a work situation, the results are likely to be variable, but very entertaining. It's true that Virgo and Sagittarius don't usually go about things in quite the same way and this can lead to a little friction now and again. All the same, there is much humour in the relationship and a common desire to keep things running smoothly. Sagittarius is far more intuitive in a work situation than Virgo, who, as a result, should take notice of what the Archer has to say. In terms of friendship, Sagittarius is one of the zodiac signs that teaches Virgo how to have a really good time. The busier and happier Virgoans are, the less time they find to worry about inconsequential matters.

A long-term attachment between Virgo and Sagittarius is almost certain to be reactive, sometimes feisty and always eventful. Virgo individuals will often playfully reproach their Sagittarius partners for some of their less-than-tidy ways, though it isn't likely that this situation ever gets beyond banter of a kind that both are likely to enjoy to the full. The relationship attracts many friends, who will be from a variety of different backgrounds.

Sagittarius can sometimes run Virgo ragged, but the sign of the Virgin is stronger than it realises and actually relishes the cut and thrust of a busy but happy life. The Archer is good for Virgo, and it shows.

 ## VIRGO meets CAPRICORN

This pairing is a recipe for a fairly quiet coming-together, though one that can be useful and productive, especially on a practical level. There is a sort of common heritage here that makes things work reasonably well because both Virgo and Capricorn are Earth signs, which means that they function well when things need to be done.

Virgo worries more than Capricorn, and the Goat doesn't always have the level of verbal skills necessary to offer the degree of reassurance that Virgo requires. Reliance is placed upon the sign of the Virgin when it comes to these individuals really keeping in touch, no matter what the relationship happens to be.

Virgo and Capricorn can achieve a great deal in work situations and are unlikely to disagree very much about the way things should be done. Progress here may be slow and steady, but it is inevitable. Both signs know that Rome wasn't built in a day and are willing to slog on relentlessly, until success becomes a matter of course. Where the signs come together in friendship there will be great loyalty, though perhaps not a tremendous measure of excitement. Both Virgo and Capricorn react best when they are supplied with the sort of stimulus that comes from more reactive zodiac signs, but this does not mean that they will find each other boring. This combination simply makes for a reflective union, which can be quite contented for both parties. However, attitude is all-important here because a little boredom could set in if Virgo and Capricorn do not maintain common friends beyond their own relationship.

The same is probably true when the two set up home together. The domestic atmosphere will be steady, and sometimes so quiet that neighbours may wonder if the pair have moved house. Within the home there will be a good deal of shared interest, particularly in the choice of fabric and furnishings. Virgo and Capricorn tend to enjoy the same sort of low-key entertainments, but in any case they will usually be found doing something constructive themselves.

 ## VIRGO meets AQUARIUS

Aquarius has what it takes to bring out the very best in Virgo, but only when and if it can be bothered to do so. Those born under the sign of the Water Bearer are deeply intuitive, a fact that won't be lost on Virgo, which has such qualities itself when it chooses to apply them. All the same, Virgo is easily puzzled by what it doesn't understand, and the very complexity of Aquarius can sometimes be a problem to an Earth sign such as the Virgin. Aquarius loves gossip, something these two zodiac signs have in common. Though neither individual could be said to be very outgoing, the two communicate almost constantly with each other and provide interest for parties far beyond themselves.

Some friction can show itself in work situations, if only because Virgo and Aquarius maintain very different ideas about the way things should be done. Aquarius may not be so meticulous as Virgo, and at the same time may show its strongly instinctive approach to life. This can cause a few problems, but it may also be the foundation of a learning process for both Virgo and Aquarius. Patience is required on both sides, as may be the case in friendship, but when this is forthcoming a useful learning process takes place that benefits both parties equally. Arguments won't occur all that often but Virgo is more likely than Aquarius to harbour resentment and so Virgoans need to speak their minds freely, though diplomatically, in this case.

A marriage or long-term personal attachment between these individuals does have a good deal going for it, though the ultimate result really depends on the ability of both parties to make allowances for each other. Aquarius isn't always particularly tidy and needs to understand that this can be a source of irritation to Virgo. The reverse is also true, and those born under the zodiac sign of the Virgin should remember that sometimes they worry about details that are really not too important.

Both signs should strive to bring out the best in each other and when they do so, each can contribute to a happy union that is capable of achieving a high degree of contentment.

VIRGO meets PISCES

This is not a particularly easy match to understand, or to be involved in, and the problem may be rooted more in Pisces than in Virgo. The sign of the Virgin is naturally inquisitive and will be fascinated by a zodiac sign as deep and difficult to penetrate as Pisces can be. Nevertheless, the latent kindness of Pisces is obvious to all, including Virgoans, who revel in the sort of attention that can come their way from this sign. There will be a certain quiet dignity in any version of this pairing, even if raw excitement is unlikely to be part of the communion. Perhaps this doesn't matter too much because both zodiac signs can be happy with their own company and, when together, they don't usually make too many waves.

Virgo and Pisces may not make the best working partners. This is not because either one is lazy or in any way unable to cope with the demands of work. A more likely explanation is that there simply isn't enough 'reaction' here. Any object that needs to move requires something to push against, but when Virgo and Pisces come together the point of resistance isn't immediately obvious. This can cause frustration, more likely for Virgo than for Pisces. Virgo doesn't always understand what Pisces is thinking, which can be infuriating to one whose whole nature is so inquisitive. In order to compensate for this fact, Pisceans need to make an extra effort to explain themselves, their thoughts and their motivations.

At the level of a permanent, domestic attachment, this can be a rather strange relationship to say the least, though this does not mean that it is impossible. Virgo and Pisces will very rarely find themselves at loggerheads. On the contrary they can live very happily together, even if some of the 'oomph' that both signs need at heart is missing in this case. Pisces shows a very warm and caring face to Virgo, who cannot fail to respond in kind. Children of this relationship may not be exposed to danger or excitement, but will be much loved.

Chapter 7
Libra

24 September to 23 October

 LIBRA meets ARIES

There is a great deal of mileage in the coming-together of the signs of the Ram and the Scales, as is so often the case in associations that involve Libra. This is because what sets Libra apart is its natural ability to get on with just about anyone. Libra is adaptable and willing to listen, and always tries to be the peacemaker. These individuals are as similar as chalk and cheese, but Aries is made gentler by its association with Libra and Libran individuals are given more opportunity to show themselves at their most dynamic when the Ram is around to lend a hand.

In any work situation, the very opposite qualities of Libra and Aries are complementary. What Aries lacks in diplomacy and tact, Libra can supply. When extra 'push' is needed, the Ram will offer it. What is more, these are people who tend to work well and happily in each other's company and are unlikely to argue. If they have family connections, Librans may consider their Aries relatives somewhat less than tactful, but they are unlikely to voice this opinion.

A personal association between Libra and Aries is not unusual and will not be difficult. On the contrary, they set up the sort of household that is always interesting and in which 'activity' tends to be the keyword. Aries may not always allow Libra enough space, for this is a sign that responds to periods of quiet contemplation. Libra on the other hand tends to be fairly quick-acting, and so is not fazed by Aries. A deep attachment is soon likely to develop here, with the Ram discovering in itself a more fulfilled and less aggressive quality, thanks to the very important lessons it learns from its Libran mate.

These two signs tend to regard objectives differently but they do at least have similar aims. Material gains tend to come from the determination of Aries, but Libra isn't far behind in its own efforts and both contribute equally to any success. When disagreements do arise, they are usually sorted out by Libra, who definitely should not hide its feelings in this match.

LIBRA meets TAURUS

If there is one word that typifies the common objective of Libra and Taurus, it is probably 'refinement'. Both these zodiac signs are ruled by the planet Venus, which brings a love of order and harmony and a common desire to keep things clean, tidy and generally peaceful. It is not at all unusual, therefore, to find these individuals coming together on all sorts of levels, because a natural affinity exists here and a sense of comfortable recognition of each other. Libra has the ability to remove some of the stubborn qualities of Taurus, whilst the Bull, by simply being itself, causes the more positive qualities of Libra to rise to the surface, making the sign show a greater degree of confidence.

The Libra–Taurus relationship generally works very well when it comes to practical matters, such as work. It's unlikely to stop there, however: these workmates are likely to choose to spend time together socially, for they relish the same sort of interests and take great delight in each other's company. Don't expect a reactive sort of attachment at any level, however. The presence of so much Venus in the match promotes quiet confidence and a common love of beauty, especially in natural surroundings.

As life partners, Libra and Taurus can easily live in the town, even though, at heart, both will probably be happier in the country. They require an uncomplicated life – the simpler the better, particularly for Taurus. Although Libra is more of a traveller than Taurus, it will generally be fairly happy to stay at home and will only occasionally feel that the more reserved side of Taurus has clipped its wings. The Bull may occasionally be jealous because Libra is so popular in company but as long as it makes some effort in this direction, Libra would be unlikely to do anything to deliberately antagonise someone it loves and respects so deeply. The sign of the Scales does need a degree of excitement and in its search for this it will most likely bring to the fore the brave and more fun-loving qualities of Taurus.

 # LIBRA meets GEMINI

Since Libra and Gemini share the same element – Air – this association has an immediate likelihood of success. All Air-sign people are adaptable and can easily change themselves to accommodate the needs of another. In the case of Libra and Gemini, the compromises are almost automatic. The really positive aspect of this pairing is that Libra and Gemini don't usually have to try very hard in order to generate affection for each other. It exists at an instinctive level and can generally be judged by the sparkle in the eyes when the two come together. Libra is naturally more refined than Gemini, who can turn a sort of vulgarity on and off like a tap. Fortunately, this only makes the average Libran laugh, for they find Gemini intelligent, reactive, stimulating and interesting.

Whatever form the coming-together of Libra and Gemini takes, the most important factor is going to be friendship. This usually exists from the word go and is the motivating force of this pairing whether the association involves work, leisure or love. There is always reaction when Libra and Gemini are present and they form a natural magnet to all manner of other people. They work best together as the nucleus of a group, and tend to 'hold court', albeit in a way that suits those knocking on their door.

When they are in a long-term relationship, Libra and Gemini must ensure that they lead a busy social life. Neither sign enjoys locking itself behind closed doors, even if Librans are naturally happier with their own company than the Twins tend to be. If there are any disagreements, these are usually short-lived because neither of these zodiac signs bears a grudge. Both are good travellers and gain a great deal from being out and about, whether that means visiting the local market or the palm-fringed beach of some exotic location.

Gemini does tend to make Libra less organised, something the Scales does not enjoy, and Librans may also find Gemini's presence tiring. Nevertheless this is generally a match that leads to contentment, happiness and a mutual enjoyment of the search for exciting horizons.

LIBRA meets CANCER

The signs of Libra and Cancer provide such pleasant people that it's hard to see how this association, at any level, can lead to anything other than overall happiness – even if there are reservations on the way. Both zodiac signs want a peaceful life and neither is inclined to cause any upsets if it can avoid it. Libra is a 'positive' zodiac sign and so will generally tend to make the running in the relationship.

At work, the two co-operate well but, as with many aspects of Libra and Cancer when together, there may be a shortage of stimulus and perhaps not the level of excitement that each can find in other zodiac combinations.

There is an essential reserve and an abiding atmosphere of quiet when Libra and Cancer spend time together. Arguments, and even deep discussions, are not particularly common and neither sign will say what it really feels unless there is some outside influence. That said, neither will realise that anything important is missing from the association. Libra and Cancer are signs that both care deeply about others, so there is a nurturing quality here that is obvious to those outside the attachment. In a family situation, these individuals are natural peacemakers and will go to almost any length to avoid any kind of argument or disagreement.

Both the Crab and the Scales can be relied upon to take the line of least resistance, and for this reason they don't move mountains when together. This need not be a problem in itself, although there may occasionally be a sort of sense that there is more to life and that some kind of excitement is being missed. Travel could be one area that would supply a little of the stimulus that the pairing lacks.

Most important of all is the attitude to families in this relationship. Libra and Cancer both love their families deeply and when together they make excellent and caring parents. However, for complete success they should try to maintain a mutual search for interests beyond the front door.

 ## LIBRA meets LEO

The association of Libra and Leo is likely to be a rip-roaring success, on almost any level. Lions possess almost everything that makes Librans feel good about thamselves and the world at large. Although considered a 'positive' zodiac sign, Libra is more affected by those around it than any other sign. Leo offers Libra the chance of excitement and in so doing allows those born under the sign of the Scales to achieve their objectives in life to the full. Libra in this relationship may not necessarily feel that anything remarkable is going on, but as a rule it is!

Libra and Leo can establish an extremely good, efficient and successful working relationship. Like all Fire signs, Leo is sometimes inclined to shoot from the hip. The presence of Libra, the diplomat, offers a calming influence and tones down some of the more strident qualities of Leo. In return, Leo offers Libra a view of its own potential and encourages those born under the Scales to take greater chances. This leads to a more confident Libran and adds to the crucible of success that is constantly bubbling and reacting. In family situations, Libra and Leo also complement each other and contribute towards creating memorable gatherings.

The Libra–Leo combination makes for one of the most reactive and happy personal attachments around, for each of these individuals has exactly what it takes to nullify the less-than-positive qualities in the other's nature. Leo encourages Libra to be less introspective and can naturally feed its inner desires to get something more out of life. The Lion also demands and gets greater constancy from Libra than many other zodiac signs could. Libra offers Leo a safe haven and is willing to accommodate and even relish Leo's natural courage and its sometimes combative ways.

What matters most is that Libra and Leo care deeply for each other. This is an attachment that is likely to be exciting, productive and long-lasting. If there is a problem at all, it comes from Leo's dominance, which may have to be curbed in this instance, since Libra is not half as compliant in the long term as it may first appear.

 ## LIBRA meets VIRGO

What works best here is Libra's natural ability to understand and defuse the more complicated qualities of the Virgoan nature. Libra is adaptable and can get away with treating Virgo in a way that virtually no other person could. Those born under the sign of the Virgin are immediately put at ease by the refined and usually jolly attitude of Libra, which Virgo doesn't find in the least intimidating or over the top. Virgo exudes a sense of order that most Librans need, even if they don't realise they do. Thus, at an instinctive level, there is great potential for shared success here.

Librans and Virgoans don't make a meal out of their common association in a work setting, even though the prognosis tends to be extremely good. These signs are complementary and though neither individual is ever going to set the world on fire, there is a quiet but definite confidence that is difficult for almost any third party to miss.

When linked by family ties, Libra and Virgo bring a sense of stability and a quiet affability that is deeply infectious. Virgo is not a natural peacemaker but can often appear to be so when Libra is present. Any sort of spat between these two individuals is extremely rare because Libra has the ability to smooth ruffled Virgoan feathers.

Long-term relationships between Libra and Virgo are extremely common, and invariably happy and successful. Gentle Libra has the ability to prevent the more nervy side of Virgo from predominating and Virgo is at its best when it feels content with life and when problems are dealt with at source. The sheer presence of someone born under the sign of the Scales makes it possible for Virgo to think and act more decisively, allowing more time for a simply enjoyment of life. The household created by these individuals would be harmonious, though perhaps a little too tidy for Libra's liking. Virgo must get used to the fact that the natural orderliness of the Scales isn't always reflected in the state of the living room carpet. Libra can bring zest to the pairing and convinces Virgo that the world is exciting, rather than specifically threatening. It is true to say that the whole is definitely greater than the sum of the parts in this pairing.

LIBRA meets LIBRA

The genuinely pleasant and easy-going nature of this relationship cannot be ignored – though neither can the fact that there are inherent problems when two people born under the zodiac sign of Libra come together. Whether the association is one of work, friendship, family attachment or love, both parties spend so much time being kind and diplomatic with each other that very little else gets done. In any other relationship, the best way to deal with this from a psychological point of view would be for Libra to find what is 'different' between itself and the other individual and to bring its powers to bear on those facts. However, when Libra meets Libra, the strategy is inclined to fail because it is too much like looking in a mirror.

In a work situation, there really isn't enough 'bite' to this association. Librans are ordered, neat and refined but they are not exactly go-getters, unless there are other people on board to make suggestions and offer options. Two Librans working alongside each other will be inclined to theorise a great deal but are most unlikely to blaze a trail with their combined success.

Probably the best association here is one of common friendship, where there is no real agenda except having a good time. This sort of Libra–Libra relationship is lightweight and almost never contentious. A family relationship will be the same and although it's true that Librans will happily side with each other when the occasion demands, the result, to the opposition, would be akin to being assaulted with a powder puff.

A Libra–Libra marriage, or in fact any form of deep, long-lasting attachment between them, will never be a particularly reactive one. The exact reverse is likely to be true. Their household will be very harmonious, but one in which very little of note take place. There will be plenty of peace and quiet, but since Libran people often tend to be absent-minded, two together could be a nightmare. In this relationship, reaction is missing, something that is hard to replace, even with simple kindness. Love will reign supreme, but is that enough?

 ## LIBRA meets SCORPIO

Libra is so adaptable that it is almost impossible to find an association that it cannot enjoy, or at the very worst cheerfully endure. Libra and Scorpio may come into the second category because there is much that sets these individuals apart. It might also be said that Scorpio is one of the few signs of the zodiac that could manage to goad Libra into argument. Libra is easy-going, kind and considerate, to such an extent that at least some Scorpio subjects will deliberately prod away until they find a chink in the Libran armour. It isn't that Scorpio is particularly vindictive or backbiting but it considers itself to be a realist, living in a flesh-and-blood world. Scorpio sometimes finds Libra too keen to bury its head in the sand – and just too nice.

Scorpio is a Water sign, which brings its own form of kindness and sympathy, but it is also ruled by fiery Mars. As a result, the Scorpion can be sarcastic, direct and biting, characteristics that it is quite likely to turn on Libra, and even in a fairly casual friendship Libra will only tolerate this behaviour for a certain period before it begins to react. 'Live and let live' is the aspect of Libran nature that Scorpio tends to push against, for it is more reactive and inclined to stick up fiercely for what it believes to be true. It is most likely then that these are individuals who probably won't form any deep sort of alliance in the first place, though at work, or in a family setting, they may not have any choice in the matter. In the latter cases, it is Scorpio who really needs to put in that extra bit of effort that can make all the difference.

Given time, Libra, with its relentless desire to balance events, can even get the better of the Scorpion, and this is, paradoxically, the reason that a deeper and more enduring relationship between these individuals may work well. Once Scorpio comes to realise that Libra is genuinely as pleasant, kind and sympathetic as it seems, a new sort of respect is likely to develop.

When any individual is 'adopted' by the Scorpion, it will go to any lengths to offer deep affection, support and enduring love. Libra then responds in kind and the seal can be set on an enduring match.

 ## LIBRA meets SAGITTARIUS

This is a joyful pairing and one that tends to work well under almost all circumstances. There is a natural and perhaps even instant affection between those born under the Scales and the happy, irrepressible Archer. Sagittarius is readily moved by the easy-going qualities of Libra and responds well to the diplomatic skills that the sign possesses. Libra in turn reacts to Sagittarius by recognising not just a kindred spirit, but one that can set it free from some of its own natural restrictions.

As friends, the two are inclined to be a good focus for others and will quite naturally form the nucleus of almost any sort of grouping. Sagittarius makes Libra slightly more competitive and encourages a greater sense of identity, which in turn deepens Libra's satisfaction with itself and the place it chooses in the world.

This is also a very good pairing in any working sense. Whilst Sagittarius has all it takes to make the necessary contacts with the world at large, Libra slips comfortably into its role as supporter and organiser. The result is very similar to that of Libra and Gemini, though in this case the relationship is more dynamic and possibly also more reactive. There is an understanding between these two signs that can work equally well in family situations, and no matter what the attachment, Libra and Sagittarius are likely to be close.

Best of all is the lifetime commitment, which only seems to get better as time goes by. There is perhaps a slight problem in that neither sign is exactly constant in a romantic sense but this won't cause problems as long as their deep-seated respect and common sense of purpose continues. Rather, it might be said that both these signs are romantic wanderers simply because they are not happy, and in this pairing they are most likely to find the happiness they seek.

Libra and Sagittarius won't get by without quite a few arguments, however, but fortunately neither party is apt to bear a grudge and both can use the relationship to hone their own respective social skills. Libra brings refinement to Sagittarius, which in return is likely to cause Libra to act and react more positively, blowing away some of Libra's tendency to sit on the fence. There are great gains here for both parties.

 ## LIBRA meets CAPRICORN

Although much quieter than some pairings in which Libra participates, the association of the Scales with the Goat has plenty of potential and can work well under many different circumstances. What Libra may not get from Capricorn, however, is the level of confidence that it needs. It is unlikely that Robinson Crusoe was a Libran, because this sign is certainly not an isolationist, and although Libra living with Capricorn isn't the same as being alone on a desert island, it may sometimes seem as if it is.

Libra and Capricorn make staunch and loyal friends. Both zodiac signs are lovers of harmony and neither wishes to make waves. Capricorn has a tremendous ability to work tirelessly towards its objectives and having Libra around can make this process just as successful and certainly more enjoyable. Libra makes Capricorn smile, something that the Goat doesn't always do as much as it might, and this fact alone means any association of this sort is particularly useful, to the Goat at least; whether Libra gets as much from the deal may be somewhat in doubt.

Family relationships of this sort are probably more or less neutral, since it's unlikely in most cases that the two signs will spend enough time together to make much of an impression either way.

It would take some years to explore fully the ultimate potential of Libra and Capricorn, so that a long-term commitment or a marriage really represents the best test of the pairing. It is likely that Libra will naturally take the lead in terms of the social aspects of life, leaving Capricorn in a fairly happy position, supporting, encouraging and acting as a safe and secure anchor. Libra may miss the cut and thrust that interaction with more positive zodiac types would bring, although this will only happen if it has previous experience that makes it realise the fact. If the Goat fails to put in the necessary effort to stimulate Libra, then some problems may follow.

Librans are patient, but they do become bored eventually and seem to be at their best when there are objectives to address. The Goat needs to reassess this relationship constantly and to make the effort that Libra requires socially.

 # LIBRA meets AQUARIUS

If everything that these two zodiac signs did went wrong, and they found their common world in tatters as a result of their own mistakes, they would probably still end up sharing a deep and abiding affection, such is the nature of Libra and Aquarius when they come together. Both these zodiac signs respond to the Air element, which makes them natural communicators, social animals and positive by inclination. Libra is fascinated by the often quirky qualities of Aquarius, which are emphasised all the more when it is not being forced down avenues that are far more conventional than it would naturally choose. Libra also allows Aquarius freedom and the Water Carrier is more than happy to run forward into the potential of each tomorrow, firmly holding Libra's hand and pulling them along too.

As friends, these two can probably not be bettered. They start with a mutual respect and a similar sense of humour. Neither takes life all that seriously and each will have other friends. There is little sense of one excluding the other in any way, and any natural jealousy or envy from either sign seems to be nullified when they come together.

Harmony reigns in families where Librans and Aquarians predominate, whilst work situations become more social commitments than chores. Libra and Aquarius bring lightness, fun and curiosity to almost anything they encounter and when they work together the result is usually a true pleasure for all concerned.

Even if these individuals had little in common in terms of basic interests, which is hardly likely to be the case, it would still be possible for them to live together happily. Domestic contentment relies, in part, on being able to cope with the way a partner squeezes the toothpaste or mows the lawn. With Libra and Aquarius there is an almost instinctive sharing of responsibility, though Libra often requires a more tidy household and one that is slightly less idiosyncratic than the Aquarian model. But these are mere details. What matters overall is the sense of happiness that radiates from the pairing and the infectious search for fun at almost all levels.

 ## LIBRA meets PISCES

Again and again in this section of the book, attention has been drawn towards the natural adaptability of the sign of Libra. This quality shows markedly when Libra comes face to face with Pisces, one of the least understood members of the zodiac family. The hard part of assessing Pisces lies in trying to fathom what makes it tick. Libra has an irrepressible curiosity and will spend days, months or years getting to the bottom of the Piscean psyche. Under certain circumstances, Pisces may resist, but it can hardly fall out with Libra on the way and, in any case, is it naturally drawn towards the friendly and approachable Libran nature.

Where friendship is concerned, Libra can have slight problems with Pisces, a naturally more reserved zodiac sign. Libra doesn't shy away from a challenge, however, and since it finds Pisces people very attractive, it will build bridges that make the attachment work. When Pisceans do commit themselves to anyone, they do so fully, and from that point on Libra can really go to work. Pisces is lacking in confidence, and so, at heart, is Libra. In helping those born under the sign of the Fishes to believe in themselves, Libra gives itself a shot of determination, so this friendship is not a one-way street by any means.

Family relationships between these zodiac sign placings are generally happy and usually serene. They share a sense of common purpose and commitment.

Pisces revels in affection, which Libra does not find in the least difficult to supply. This forms the basis of any attachment deeper than a simple friendship. Libra is open-minded and generous, qualities that are typified by the sign of the Fishes. Pisces might not always be able to offer the degree of diversion or interest that Libra requires, however, and this could be a slight stumbling-block.

It is probably fair to say that this romance would work best for Libra if it were the sign's first serious encounter. If not, Libra may compare the Pisces type with more dominant individuals and will find it somewhat lacking as a result. Generally speaking, happiness would reign in this household, even if Libra has to suppress its natural tendencies a little in order to make the best of the pairing.

Chapter 8
Scorpio
24 October to 22 November

 SCORPIO meets ARIES

Despite the fact that Scorpio is a Water sign and therefore tends to be introverted, it won't stand being bullied. It has the same planetary ruler as Aries and though Mars displays itself very differently through each of these zodiac signs, its presence is marked all the same. Aries seeks to get to its destinations through determination and force, whereas Scorpio refuses to be pushed and makes a formidable enemy if too much pressure is forthcoming.

Scorpio is a very closed sign, secret and difficult to understand. Aries will find this awkward to deal with and is inclined to run out of patience quickly when dealing with the Scorpion. Attitudes differ, and yet there is a nucleus of understanding that can bring a distinct passion to this association.

When working towards common objectives, Scorpio and Aries can complement each other well, and a deep and abiding respect then tends to develop. Friends from these zodiac placings will probably enjoy different stimuli but both can be sporting by nature and anxious to win. Family ties carrying these connections are apt to be reactive, though the inherent loyalty of Scorpio and Aries will come to the fore when an outside threat is evident.

Because of the latent passion of Scorpio, together with an Aries determination to be the world's best lover, this matching does happen frequently at a romantic level. However, whether it is destined to last is totally dependent on the attitude of the individuals concerned. Aries needs to learn to tone down its dynamic ways and to use subtlety. Scorpions should be prepared to speak more about their feelings, as well as being willing to abandon their slight tendency to sulk and to bear grudges.

This pairing can prove to be extremely interesting. Their overriding commitment to family will beat that of any other zodiac sign combination, together with a very marked ability to make money together. Changes need to be rung, however, and Scorpio must be prepared to show its social side.

SCORPIO meets TAURUS

From the outset it has to be said that this is, potentially at least, a generally good pairing. The only general problem stems from the fact that both Scorpio and Taurus are 'fixed' zodiac signs. This means, in essence, that they can both be extremely stubborn. To the Scorpio and Taurean association, this can prove to be either a very good thing or a disaster. If they both have the ability to concentrate and to push through to a specific common destination, no matter what the obstacle, all should be well. It is really only when the Scorpion and the Bull are opposed in their plans or wishes that things tend to go somewhat astray.

Both these zodiac signs are very careful and will tend to have a similar sort of attitude to life. In a work setting, they can both be relied upon to get on with the task in hand and they will co-operate well, just as long as there is no element of competition. Friends from this zodiac sign combination are common, though they are not generally to be found whooping it up: when together, Scorpio and Taurus show the quieter side of their respective natures. That said, Taurus is naturally more outgoing than Scorpio and finds it easier to socialise under certain circumstances.

The real drawback to this association lies in the fact that both Scorpio and Taurus only give of their very best when associated with zodiac signs that are more dynamic and extrovert. They need the presence of such people to act as a stimulus and without them this could be a rather quiet attachment.

On a personal level, this relationship brings great loyalty and a common respect that could hardly be bettered. Since Taurus is happy with a quiet and refined sort of life, it could be quite content with Scorpio, but this may turn out to be the sort of relationship in which the respective partners often get on with doing their own thing. The scope for genuine and deep-seated passion inherent in this pairing should not be dismissed, however, nor the tremendous ability to work towards common objectives where family matters are concerned. There can be great intensity and a mutual encouragement.

 # SCORPIO meets GEMINI

Whilst the sign of Gemini is known for its adaptability, the same cannot be generally said for Scorpio. As a result, much of the running here, at almost any level, will be made by the sign of the Twins and immediately there are going to be certain problems and restraints.

Gemini is deeply intuitive and tries to establish a contact with others almost straight away. This will be almost impossible to achieve with Scorpio.

Those viewing this relationship from the outside will find it odd and quirky. This does not mean that it is a bad match at all levels, however.

In a working association, Scorpio has the ability to concentrate and doesn't mind deferring to the more agile and mentally motivated Gemini because it doesn't often feel threatened. Gemini will rarely try to bully, and that fact appeals to the Scorpion.

In a family relationship, Gemini takes a very much more casual approach than the Scorpion, who is inclined to stick to its loved ones like glue. However, Scorpio does respect the ability of the Twins to get on with almost anyone and can learn a great deal from Gemini's winning ways. Basic attitudes to life may differ and Scorpio is inclined to believe that Gemini is rather too flippant and takes a rather too casual approach to many situations.

This is not a particularly common romantic pairing. Gemini absolutely demands diversity and change, neither of which is high on the list of Scorpio's needs. Social impulses tend to be somewhat different, with Gemini often wanting to be out there in the world, making friends and having fun. Scorpio meanwhile is rather more serious, loves to stay at home and exhibits a tendency towards secretive ways that Gemini finds to be puzzling. It can't be denied that the two signs are good for each other, for there is a cross-fertilisation of ideas that can be most useful. What seems to be in doubt is whether either individual will want to put in the effort necessary to make this alliance work in the first place.

Scorpio can teach capricious Gemini a great deal about genuine passion but finds Gemini difficult to understand.

 ## SCORPIO meets CANCER

The fact that both Scorpio and Cancer are Water signs can be the saving grace of this attachment. Cancer is perhaps the more reserved of the two, or at least that's how it appears when they get together.

An understanding of the creatures these zodiac signs are named after can be most illuminating in this case. The Scorpion is not an animal that goes looking for trouble, though when faced with confrontation it will take on opponents many times its size. The Crab, meanwhile, survives by retreating into its shell if confronted. Even at the level of friendship, therefore, it appears that Scorpio is going to have to take command, but it must be said that both these zodiac signs tend to be at their best when faced with individuals who are less alike than the Scorpion and the Crab.

When it comes to family attachments, there could hardly be a better-suited couple than this. Both have a great fondness for home and family and each is deeply loyal in its own way. Their mental motivation is similar, as are their personal interests, with the exception that the Scorpion is a good deal more competitive than the Crab.

These individuals would work harmoniously together, though the working environment would probably be quiet and hardly reactive.

As life partners, Scorpio and Cancer usually get on rather well, although this is a distinctly quiet relationship. Neighbours of the Scorpio–Cancer couple will hardly know that they exist, yet within the home there will be a deep-seated contentment and probably a fair degree of passion too. Arguments will not be frequent, for Cancer will most often defer to the wishes of Scorpio before any potential situation gets out of hand. Cancer doesn't find the depth of the Scorpio nature at all difficult and there is a commonness of purpose that could set this apart as a very happy and enduring combination.

The most important motivating factor of all for these two signs is their commitment to family members and the willing sacrifices they will make on behalf of loved ones generally.

SCORPIO meets LEO

Scorpio and Leo do not make a particularly likely pairing, except on those occasions when circumstances or family ties more or less force them together. The basic problem, and it exists at almost every level, is the fact that both these individuals come from 'fixed' zodiac signs. Whereas other sign combinations of very different sorts may come together out of a common need to learn, Scorpio and Leo just rub each other up the wrong way, so in many cases the match doesn't really have the chance to get started. In a way that is a pity because although the motivating factors are rather different in each case, Scorpio and Leo do have a good deal to learn from each other.

At work, Scorpio is likely to find Leo too showy, sometimes overbearing and perhaps a little pompous. Leo sees the Scorpio as dark, difficult to penetrate and inclined to be rather sulky. This is not a good start. Only with supreme effort will these individuals get to know each other well, allowing a greater degree of co-operation to develop, followed by understanding and then affection.

The same is generally true in family situations. Leo is tremendously loyal but is not tied to the idea of family commitments in the same way that Scorpio tends to be.

It is not particularly common to find Scorpio and Leo people living together for any length of time, unless forced to do so by circumstance. With a degree of divergence from type in either case, the relationship can work well, but if both individuals are absolutely typical of their zodiac sign, they probably would not get together willingly in the first place.

Confrontation is always a possibility, with Scorpio often defending itself before it is attacked and Leo feeling somewhat threatened by the deep and secretive Scorpion. With a monumental effort, however, barriers can be torn down and each person concerned can get to know the other properly. When this happens there is passion, commitment, interest and understanding but, sadly, in this case it's all too rare. Leo is also probably too social for Scorpio to cope with and in terms of natural personal interests there is also something of a divergence.

 ## SCORPIO meets VIRGO

This is a relationship that has a great deal going for it, and the possibilities can shine out at every level. There is always a good chance of success when a 'fixed' and a 'mutable' sign come together and it is particularly evident in this case. Virgo has enough depth of its own not to be intimidated by the same quality in Scorpio, and yet has a lighter touch with the world at large. It is more inclined to be sociable and to talk. These Mercurial tendencies look attractive when viewed from the perspective of Scorpio and, almost paradoxically, Virgo has the ability to lighten the Scorpio nature.

There is great practical potential in this association, so that business interests are shared well and dealt with capably. Add to this the fact that here we have two people who don't find it at all difficult to rub along at a personal level and the prognosis for financial success tends to be extremely promising. A friendship that goes far beyond the environs of work can develop, for Scorpio and Virgo are interested in the same sort of things and will rarely be short of something to talk about. It would be true to say that, at almost any level, the world at large may fail to see what is going on in this attachment but that doesn't matter in the least as long as the individuals concerned remain content.

The possibilities for romance here are also extremely promising. Both these zodiac signs are capable of passion, with Scorpio leading the field and bringing Virgo to a better understanding of its own emotional reserves. Comfort and security are equally important to both the Scorpio and the Virgoan, with the need for a stable and successful home environment also predominating in each case. Happiness will come through common incentives, good co-operation and a developing ability to offer mutual help and support.

All in all, this zodiac sign combination is of great benefit to both individuals and helps to unlock the latent potential that typifies Scorpio as much as it does Virgo. The union can become so deep that the outside world can sometimes be excluded, however, and this is something that needs to be guarded against.

 # SCORPIO meets LIBRA

Scorpio needs to work at this relationship much harder than Libra. Those born under the zodiac sign of the Scales are easy-going and will do almost anything for the sake of peace and harmony. Although this is also true for Scorpio in its association with some individuals, the same may not be the case in its contacts with Libra.

Scorpio can, on occasions, be quite sarcastic and it also considers itself a realist. The happy and settled world of Libra doesn't look at all real to Scorpio, which is inclined to torment Libra as a result. However, it is not difficult to avoid this course of action and if Scorpio comes to understand that most Librans really are as pleasant as they appear to be, harmony could be the result.

Family relationships between these two signs may be somewhat fraught on occasions because it's a fact that Scorpio can manage to annoy even the normally placid Libra.

At work, the two signs are hardly likely to co-operate greatly and have different strategies to consider. Out-and-out dislike will probably not be the result, but rather a mutual agreement to stay apart as much as circumstances allow. This is a shame because Libra has much that Scorpio needs in terms of social skills, whilst those born under the sign of the Scales can gain from Scorpio's 'bite' and ultimate determination.

If the initial barriers can be broken down – and this generally has to be undertaken by Scorpio – the two people concerned may eventually find happiness together. Libra has winning ways and its own form of persistence may well pay off in the end.

Together, Scorpio and Libra will opt for a tidy and generally well-ordered household. With this combination we could expect a gradually developing respect that may, in the fullness of time, turn into deep, enduring love. Neither of these people is likely to foresee this end result, however, and it is true that, at first sight, Scorpio and Libra really don't appear to have very much in common, which is why this combination does tend to be fairly rare in the romantic stakes. Nevertheless, it only takes a very slight divergence from the expected behaviour of either person for the prognosis to change markedly.

SCORPIO meets SCORPIO

With almost any pairing in which the individuals come from the same zodiac sign, the prognosis is usually either excellent or disastrous. When Scorpio and Scorpio come together, the former is much more likely. The main reason for this lies in the fact that Scorpio is so difficult to understand. There is usually a long apprenticeship involved in getting to know what really makes the Scorpion tick, but this is not the case when two come together. A common understanding gets the pair off to a good start at any level, and increases the chances of overall success.

At heart, most Scorpio types don't care for themselves all that much, though when confronted with the best of what they can be, reflected back from another person, the level of self-appreciation increases markedly. With a similarity of working techniques and objectives, Scorpio work colleagues can co-operate fully and will toil away relentlessly towards a common objective. The association won't be particularly quiet either, if only because Scorpio when faced with itself doesn't feel in the least threatened and so is likely to be more voluble and naturally friendly.

This pairing can be the very best family and friendship tie of them all. Here we would find staunch loyalty, great mutual support and a potential for humour that often passes Scorpio by in its association with other zodiac signs.

When Scorpio people come together in a romantic entanglement we can expect passion with a capital 'P'. Only those born under this sign can come close to understanding the depths from which the Scorpion dredges up its reserves of love. Whether the two Scorpio parties show this burning passion to the world at large will really depend on the circumstances of the life they chose to share.

Scorpio has a secretive, closed nature, which can be something akin to a vast and mysterious building, the door of which is almost always kept locked. When two Scorpios unite, the portals may be thrown open for the whole world to see.

 ## SCORPIO meets SAGITTARIUS

Scorpio tends to be attracted almost instinctively to the winning nature of Sagittarius and respects the way it has with the world. The latent dominance of the Scorpion, often expressed in strange ways because it is basically an introverted sign, is less likely to surface when the sign comes up against a Fire-ruled individual such as Sagittarius. In addition, the Archer does not usually take itself or anyone else very seriously, an attitude that can suit Scorpio down to the ground.

Scorpio is often inclined to be quiet but finds this difficult when confronted with chatty Sagittarius. When in a work situation, Sagittarius will do most of the talking but can be more 'directed' and regulated by having Scorpio around. Perhaps surprisingly, this adds to the overall success of the enterprise, since the presence of Scorpio allows Sagittarius a greater latitude, which reflects in the strength of the partnership.

Within the family, Sagittarius keeps an eye on quieter Scorpio and seems instinctively to understand the depths of this hard-to-fathom individual. In return the Scorpion offers great commitment and support of a practical nature.

Overall, this combination bodes well for wedded bliss, because here we have a situation where both parties can work to the best of their ability. The Archer may constantly have to demonstrate more loyalty than it is used to, if only because Scorpio is capable of being very jealous indeed. This said, Sagittarius considerably lightens the load of the Scorpion, and gradually nudges it towards a more liberal point of view, which in turn brings a deeper form of contentment.

Certainly there will be passion here, and possibly a very good physical relationship. Arguments will crop up from time to time, though surprisingly few, considering the natural proclivities of these two zodiac signs. Smouldering Scorpio simply doesn't get a chance to burst into flames when faced by disarming Sagittarius. The end result can be deep and enduring affection.

SCORPIO meets CAPRICORN

Here we have another potentially good match for Scorpio. From the outset it has to be said that this is not going to be the most reactive relationship around, but on a practical level, and when it comes to plumbing the depths of these two mysterious natures, the results can be very good indeed.

Capricorn is basically a no-nonsense sign, or at least that's what the Goat would have us believe. 'What you see is what you get', it tells us by its every action. In reality, however, Capricorn is a deep thinker. True, it tends not to have the same sort of emotional responses as Scorpio, but that doesn't mean that it can't acquire them. Scorpio is very supportive of Capricorn's efforts to get things done and, being naturally lazy on occasions, will be happy to sit and watch. Thus at the level of work or friendship Scorpio wins out because Capricorn likes to 'do', whilst the Scorpion is often happy to 'observe'.

Family ties of this sort should be fairly strong and enduring because Scorpio and Capricorn discover quickly how to get along well together.

When it comes to a deeper and more lasting sort of attachment, the one and only problem is working out how it might come about. Neither of these individuals has a natural 'chat up' line, though assuming that they do get together, the end product tends to be very happy and singularly successful. Capricorn loves to make the Scorpion happy and that brings out the best in the Mars-ruled Water sign, whose reserves of passion are then forthcoming. This might intimidate some zodiac signs but is hardly likely to faze Capricorn, who manages to take almost anything in its stride.

The domestic situation will be slow and steady, and social trends may not be too evident. The most likely place to find this couple is either in the summer garden or else curled up together in front of the television. Nevertheless Capricorn likes to keep busy in a practical sense, which doesn't trouble Scorpio at all. Family ties will be important to this couple, though flexibility needs to be present when they take to rearing children, who could feel somewhat stifled.

 ## SCORPIO meets AQUARIUS

This is a strange attachment, though one that might work extremely well. Aquarians have an almost irrepressible curiosity and they are especially fascinated by Scorpio individuals, who they quite simply want to analyse. Since Scorpio is quite happy as long as someone cares, this coming-together can suit both parties equally.

Aquarius is sometimes depicted as an unfaithful zodiac sign, a suggestion that doesn't merely apply to romance. Aquarians have many friends and, dodging about between them as they do, they can seem fickle. Actually, it's all a matter of curiosity. Scorpio provides Aquarius with an almost endless source of study and conjecture. It can therefore be seen that, from the outset, Scorpio captures the Aquarian interest – and tends to hang on to it. Aquarius is kind, giving, original and, when necessary, quite strong. Scorpio is emotional in a smouldering sort of way, can be loyal beyond belief and has a natural instinct to protect. Together, Scorpio and Aquarius form the weirdest sort of interlocking that could be imagined, and yet it works.

Expect a quirky atmosphere in this couple's domestic situation. Even the very building they choose to inhabit may be out of the ordinary in some way, if only because Scorpio revels in the 'oddness' of Aquarius and comes to embrace it. This is good for the Scorpion, who has less time to worry about things and more moments to display aspects of its own nature that, in some cases, never surface at all. There can be a deep, though rather off-beat, love and certainly plenty of mutual affection. At its most exaggerated this can seem like some sort of 'Alice in Wonderland' scenario. It's strange, even weird and yet it seems to work well and can creak along erratically for a lifetime.

This will be an entertaining couple to know socially and one that will rear an equally original family. There is also strong creativity present and perhaps a common desire to plumb artistic depths. Rules and regulations, usually kicked against by both these zodiac signs, won't apply within this common space.

SCORPIO meets PISCES

From the very beginning we have to realise that Scorpio and Pisces are both Water signs, so there is bound to be a sort of understanding and mutual sympathy in this relationship that offers the pairing a much better than average chance of success. Scorpio and Pisces do not provide the most exciting combination, but at any level the depth of mutual respect can provide a level of happiness that flows out into the world, making Scorpio and Pisces good to be around.

Scorpio rarely shows its more caustic or sarcastic side when with Pisces, who is naturally disarming and, though itself deep, very genuine. This appeals to the Scorpion and certainly helps to create a potentially happy working relationship. Its association with Pisces forces Scorpio to take the lead, and particularly so when the rest of the world is watching.

In a family situation, Water-sign relationships such as this invariably provide a supportive environment, which looks particularly attractive to outsiders. The association takes no account of the age of the parties involved, and no matter what the attachment may be, it simply works, usually without complication and at an instinctive level.

Scorpio and Pisces are frequently found setting up home together. There is a naturalness in this pairing that makes for a very comfortable life and one that might be the very best for both parties. It is true that neither Scorpio nor Pisces is 'stretched' in this union, certainly not to the extent that either might be by more positive zodiac types. In all probability there won't be any natural desire for either party to push itself further than is necessary. But, in any case, when together, the efforts of both Scorpio and Pisces are spent supporting each other and, in particular, children, the natural result of this loving union. If outsiders tend to comment that Scorpio and Pisces are somehow too comfortable, this is probably because those making the comments have never managed to discover anything as near to perfection for themselves.

Scorpio and Pisces form a union built on understanding and there is nothing in the least artificial about it. With these individuals, what you see is truly what you get.

Chapter 9
Sagittarius
23 November to 21 December

 SAGITTARIUS meets ARIES

This is bound to be a reactive association and generally turns out to be quite successful. There is going to be a competitive edge in any attachment and a desire by each to be top dog. Since both the zodiac signs in question are well used to any sort of competition, this fact alone will not stand in the way of a generally positive coming-together.

As co-workers Sagittarius and Aries can do really well. There is great dynamism present in these two Fire-sign individuals, together with a common desire to win. The Archer and the Ram have great respect for each other in the market place and should find it easy to achieve ultimate objectives together.

In any group of friends who are determined to paint the town red, it's a fair bet that there will be a smattering of Sagittarius and Aries individuals present. Both signs love to have a good time, especially together, though things can get a little out of hand when each is trying to better the other. In most situations Aries manages to get ahead, but this isn't always the case because Sagittarius is quick-thinking and can sometimes outsmart the Ram, though invariably in a good-natured way. However, if the people concerned definitely don't like each other, then sparks can really fly.

Sagittarius and Aries may be slightly less inclined to find themselves living together in a personal attachment. If they do, the relationship is always going to be eventful. Great happiness can be the result but there is usually an 'edge' to the relationship that could make the rest of the world think that this is a boxing match, rather than a marriage. Nothing could be further from the truth and both Sagittarius and Aries are happy to be competitors as well as lovers. Two Fire signs of this sort bring great commitment to home and family but can spend as much time away from it as much as in it. Travel is important to both signs, who can also co-operate well as life partners and business associates – something that is not uncommon here.

Don't expect a quiet and uneventful relationship to develop with this couple – but there will be great passion and a genuine joy that is bound to seem infectious when viewed by the rest of the world. That said, there will also be times when the vases are flying and all is not sweetness and light.

 ## SAGITTARIUS meets TAURUS

Seen from the perspective of Sagittarius, there is great potential in this relationship. Actually, this is true for both parties, though with a few reservations coming from the direction of Taurus. What matters most about this association is more to do with the differences between the zodiac signs in question than with their similarities. Sagittarius is a zany go-getter, always on the move and determined to have a good time at all costs. Taurus is slower and more methodical. Between the two lies a wealth of possibilities and a potential for a sensible compromise that assists both.

Sagittarius and Taurus should have little trouble working together. This might be the ideal partnership because the Archer is so good at talking, whilst the Bull is excellent at actually getting things done. Left to its own devices Taurus won't be inclined to take too many chances but the Archer offers the sort of incentives that ensure forward movement.

The same is generally true in friendship. The eventual closeness of this pair simply can't be underestimated. Part of this has to do with the fact that Sagittarius and Taurus are both naturally affable zodiac signs. What Taurus lacks in progress, Sagittarius possesses. Meanwhile, the Bull is refined and steady, both qualities that the Archer needs to foster, and alongside Taurus it can do so.

As life partners, this pair should prove to be successful. The usual tendency of Sagittarius to wander when things get tedious is less likely to be an issue. Taurus knows how to keep its mate and although not the most progressive of the zodiac signs, it is adaptable enough to stay beside Sagittarius on the roller-coaster that is the Archer's life. Sagittarius should always be aware of the stubborn side of Taurus, which is legendary. However, it is possible that this can be turned to the advantage of the relationship and if anyone can arrange that, the Archer can.

Here we find friendliness, affection, co-operation and superb mutual support. True, there are times when these zodiac signs will be at odds with each other, but this worries the Bull more than the Archer.

SAGITTARIUS meets GEMINI

This is likely to be one of the most reactive pairings that the zodiac can offer. Sagittarius and Gemini are opposite signs in the zodiac and yet, in many respects, they show a very similar face to the world. At the level of simple liking, there should not be any real difficulty. Both these signs throw up friendly people who have a desire to get on with the world at large. However, what might prove to be a problem at any level is the need of both Sagittarius and Gemini to be the centre of attention. This can be difficult and, under certain circumstances, may even turn out to make the relationship impossible to maintain.

There's nothing routine about either the Archer or those born under the Twins. If working together means one or other having to make the tea or file away documents, both of these individuals would expend more energy getting out of the task than they would simply doing it. What is certainly not missing here is a great sense of impish fun. It will be a working environment full of practical jokes and quick, reactive banter – more like a double act than a working relationship.

At the level of friendship, Sagittarius and Gemini probably won't function very readily except as part of a larger group. When alone, almost paradoxically, Sagittarius and Gemini will find the quieter side of each other's nature and this could come as something of a shock to both. There is depth to both signs, but it shows all too rarely.

Sagittarius and Gemini as lovers is certainly a sight to see. From the start, this romance is going to be hearts, flowers, effusive poetry and a common desire to please that knows no bounds. Underlying this is a sort of competition, which is typical of both individuals. Long-term prospects might not be quite so good. If, as suggested, this coming-together is a double act, one partner will have to be prepared to play the straight man in order for it to succeed in the long term. It is difficult to see who this might be. But even if things don't work out, these individuals should still end up being friends because neither has the slightest idea how to bear a grudge.

This pairing can endure, and when it does so this is thanks to the natural adaptability of both Sagittarius and Gemini.

 ## SAGITTARIUS meets CANCER

Sagittarius is one of the most versatile, restless and loveable of the zodiac signs. These are qualities that immediately seem attractive to Cancer, itself a much quieter and less confident type. For this reason a short-term association between the two can provide a very happy interlude. Only when there is continuity does each sign begin to have a bearing on the other. Under almost all circumstances, the level of hero-worship that passes from the Crab to the Archer initially excludes very much input from Cancer's true nature. However, with the passing of time it will show.

These are two zodiac signs that quite naturally like each other. The Archer is not half as confident as it appears to be and really does need constant reassurance. This is something Cancer can offer, especially in a working relationship. Cancer is not so progressive, but it does have the ability to work long and hard, achieving its objectives as a result of persistence and patience. This can contrast well with the go-getting tendencies of the Archer. Simply getting on together in a day-to-day sense is not a problem. Sagittarius knows how to make a fuss of the Crab, which responds in kind by being very protective of the impish and capricious Sagittarian.

Friendships are common between these types, though they are less likely to show themselves through their chosen forms of entertainment. Sagittarius wants to paint the town red. Cancer may choose to go along for a while but is really more of a home-bird at heart.

In terms of romance, the initial stages of this combination can be very good. Sagittarius offers the compliments and Cancer accepts them, willingly and gracefully. But what the Archer needs more than anything is stimulation and there may be times when the Crab finds this difficult to offer in sufficient quantity. If the Cancerian involved is the sort of individual who is helped to learn and grow by this attachment, the prognosis is better because on the way it can also do much to curb the tendency of Sagittarius to fly too high.

Expect a reactive and interesting household. There ought to be few arguments, if only because the Crab won't be drawn into them.

 ## SAGITTARIUS meets LEO

There is certainly no lack of reaction here. Both Sagittarius and Leo are Fire signs and that means that each is a natural leader in its own right. There is always going to be a good deal of competition displayed by this pairing, though potentially a high degree of natural friendship too. In fact it might be at the level of friendship that the Archer and the Lion find their greatest common ground. Friends are not together all the time and the natural reaction that takes place in this pairing is wonderful but it probably needs to be balanced by times spent with other, less reactive types.

Both the Archer and the Lion have a great zest for life and this will show when they come together in any sort of work situation. The friendship that ensues can extend far beyond the place of work but tends to display itself in more or less the same way socially. Both signs have plenty of energy and are quite happy to dance until dawn. They have complementary characteristics too. Leo has greater staying-power and more solid determination. This is balanced by the Sagittarian desire to get things done and the Archer probably makes the better 'front man' (or woman) of the two. Mutual support isn't difficult, except when both decide that they want to rule the roost.

This may not be a natural pairing for conjugal bliss, but this does not mean that it will fail to work. The pace of life will be fast, but as long as both parties have the necessary energy to cope with this, the association can be stimulating, eventful and usually quite happy. There are bound to be arguments because the Archer and the Lion both seek to compete. At the same time there will be a greater degree of loyalty from Sagittarius than might usually be expected. Leo can sometimes be jealous, which may rock the relationship, especially since the Archer is not the most constant individual. At a domestic level, clear lines of demarcation will have to be established. Both signs are 'workers', so that the washing, cooking, cleaning and ironing will seem a piece of cake to both.

 SAGITTARIUS meets VIRGO

A psychologist, taking each of these individuals at face value, might well declare that this potential relationship has little viability. In general, he or she would be wrong. Although it might appear that Sagittarius and Virgo have little in common, both these zodiac signs possess a quirky side and therefore neither necessarily reacts according to expectations. Virgo seems to love the more brash and chatty side of Sagittarius and will talk more itself when in the company of the irrepressible Archer. Neither is there any lack of possible topics of conversation – Sagittarius and Virgo share the ability to pick up information from the world around them and, together, can chat about it for hours.

Virgo is not too keen on the way Sagittarius organises itself – or rather the way it doesn't. One might assume that this could create a degree of friction, but what is more likely to happen is that the Virgoan individual will simply follow the Archer round and clear up the mess that is being created. Why Sagittarius can get away with this sort of behaviour, when virtually no other zodiac sign could, is something of a mystery. The Archer simply has something about it that Virgo finds extremely attractive.

As friends, Sagittarius and Virgo can spend endless hours together. The Archer has the ability to make the Virgoan nature much more flexible and those born under the sign of the Virgin are less inclined to stick close to home when the Archer is present. The two will discover common objectives and fascination follows.

Romantically speaking, the potential is also good. Sagittarius likes to be looked after, something that the Virgo half of the match understands. But the Archer is not half so superficial as it at first appears, and so it will become more responsive to the needs of its Virgoan partner as time goes by. The simple fact is that, with a few reservations, Sagittarius and Virgo have the ability to bring out the better qualities latent within each other. The association should be reasonably good from a financial point of view because Virgo tends to hoard.

There can be great happiness here.

 ## SAGITTARIUS meets LIBRA

Whilst Libra is a natural fence-sitter, Sagittarius definitely is not. There will probably be an instant rapport here and the Scales may be able to show the Air-sign qualities that, under some circumstances, it is inclined to repress. Sagittarius allows Libra a great deal of scope and offers plenty of opportunities for the Libran's natural refinement to be used to the advantage of the Archer.

Friendship is almost a certainty for this pair. Both tend to be cheerful types who enjoy the same sort of entertainment and love to travel. Although fond of fun, Sagittarius and Libra can both work hard, specifically because, when together, the whole thing seems to be a great deal of fun too.

Family relationships of this sort ensure a sense of entertainment and since both these zodiac signs take no notice of age, the generation gap is not a problem for either. The Archer and those born under the sign of the Scales both come from positive zodiac signs, though Libra would generally, especially in social matters, defer to Sagittarius, who is irrepressible, charming and full of enterprise.

There is usually very little problem when the Archer and the Libran get to grips at a personal level. This is a romance full of promise. Neither sign is inclined to take itself too seriously and so a bright and breezy sort of relationship tends to be the result. Sagittarius increases the confidence that Libra feels for life and the very dependence and trust that Libra holds out for this union is likely to force the Archer down a faithful and steadfast path.

Despite having its fair share of tiffs, this attachment could very easily stand the test of time, bringing more than a sparkle to the lives of all those it encounters. This is also a good pairing when it comes to a developing sense of refinement. Sagittarians and Librans tend to make happy, relaxed parents with an open attitude.

Most of all, these individuals love to have a good time and they encourage others to join them. Routine, they believe, is for the birds and they maintain a common need for action.

SAGITTARIUS meets SCORPIO

Here we find two radically different sorts of people. Sagittarius and Scorpio tend to look at virtually every aspect of life from almost completely opposite perspectives but they do still have a great deal to offer each other, just as long as they get off to a good start.

Scorpio is difficult to get to know well and this may be the first stumbling-block in this relationship. Everything about the Archer is turned outwards, to the world at large. This is a sign that, for most of its life, retains the inquisitive nature of a small child. But, also like a youngster, the Archer isn't very interested in plumbing the depths of any situation. As a result, it may never come to understand the most important qualities that the Scorpio individual possesses. The Archer does have the ability to lighten the load of the more naturally serious Scorpion and is usually appreciated for its efforts. Scorpio loves to be paid compliments and to receive the sort of attention that the Archer deals out to just about anyone – simply because that's the way it functions.

The two have the capacity to work well together, just as long as they don't attempt any sort of role reversal. Scorpio is the better organiser here, whilst Sagittarius functions at a social level.

It takes the Archer quite a while to realise how loyal, sincere, persevering and magnetic Scorpio can be. For this reason, the attraction between them may not be instant but it will probably develop because Scorpio is one of the sexiest of all zodiac signs. Sagittarius is drawn into the sizzling depths of Scorpio, from which it will rarely want to escape. Since the Scorpion loves with all its heart and soul and Sagittarius has a great need to be adored, there is a strong chance that this pairing could endure. One particular problem might be the fact that Sagittarius has an irrepressible need for change and diversity, which can go against the grain for Scorpio, who is more inclined to take delight at home.

Although this isn't the most common romantic pairing, it does have certain advantages and can grow more convincing with the passing of time. Be ready for a few fireworks on the way, however.

 ## SAGITTARIUS meets SAGITTARIUS

Fasten your safety belt and prepare for a wild and wonderful ride. There may not be much depth to this pairing, no matter what the relationship is, but it's a roller-coaster ride that both parties are quite likely to enjoy. Sagittarius is probably the most sociable and gregarious of all the signs and, unlike some others, it usually adores being in the company of its own type.

Friendships formed when Archer meets Archer can be brief, though under certain circumstances they can span a lifetime. To get in under the brash exterior of this sign isn't easy – in fact some unkind souls would say that there's nothing to discover, although, of course, this isn't the case. However, one Sagittarian associating with another definitely has a distinct advantage when it comes to plumbing the depths of this zany and puzzling sign.

Family pairs of this type, especially if they are siblings, will often fight like cat and dog. It isn't possible for more than one person to rule the roost, and this is what lies at the heart of the problem. As they become adults, the situation will change, bringing both liking and loyalty, together with the sort of mutual support that can only develop through common understanding.

Two Sagittarians will probably embark on a more personal relationship at the drop of a hat, for this sign functions on impulse. This will therefore be an attachment with never a dull moment and one that might easily offer a great deal in the way of mutual fulfilment and satisfaction. Some caution is necessary, however. The rate of failed relationships is high for Sagittarius, and presumably twice as high when two Archers come together. On the other hand, the level of joy and the natural sense of freedom that is present when Sagittarius meets its counterpart may be enough to ensure a higher degree of constancy from both parties.

The practicalities of life could be something of a problem but with their ability to co-operate, this couple may become millionaires – or paupers, though it probably won't matter. Friends will be shared.

SAGITTARIUS meets CAPRICORN

The Sagittarius and Capricorn pairing comes close to being the ideal combination of theory and practice. Sagittarius is a great dreamer and schemer. It isn't tardy when it comes to putting plans into action either, though it lacks the practical know-how and general common sense that is so typical of Capricorn. There is a natural and complementary balance between the signs and as a rule a definite liking.

The Archer loves to play the field in any social situation. It might appear that Capricorn, a naturally slower and steadier sort of sign, would not have what it takes to capture the attention of a sign such as Sagittarius, which is always looking for a new opportunity. But the Archer is no fool and appreciates that it can achieve even more in life if it is allied with a more grounded sort of individual, as typified by the Goat.

In friendship, the Goat defers to the Archer socially but learns a great deal about enjoying itself, whilst at the same time offering the Archer a pal with greater depth and a wealth of solutions to most of life's little problems. Both signs have a great sense of humour, even if that of Capricorn is dryer and less immediate.

As life partners, Sagittarius and Capricorn are likely to be happy. There is a strong sense of reliance in the making here, brought about by two very different individuals who have what it takes to learn and grow in each other's company. The Archer is less likely to be flirtatious or to play the field in this union, particularly since Capricorn is inclined to offer a depth to Sagittarius that it fails to find in certain other relationships.

Both signs want to get on in life, Sagittarius through its ingenuity and ability to present itself well, Capricorn more by its work behind the scenes, where it is willing to act as a prop and occasionally as a restraint. With a little mutual admiration thrown in for good measure, we find in this association most of the requisites for lasting happiness, a commodity that isn't always easy for Sagittarius to find.

SAGITTARIUS meets AQUARIUS

Aquarius is probably exactly the right sort of zodiac sign to complement Sagittarius. The Water Bearer is an Air sign, whilst Sagittarius glories under the Fire element. This is a combination that generally works quite well, though on a superficial, rather than deep or emotional, level. Sagittarius may well be surprised at just how 'off the wall' Aquarius can be, for when the sign is working to its full capacity it can be even madder than the Archer.

When it comes to success in business, the Archer could do much worse than to team up with an intelligent Aquarian. Toiling together, these zodiac signs probably have what it takes to move swiftly along the path to success. On the way, they are unlikely to fall out to any degree. Aquarius is a deeply mentally motivated sign. It wants to know why people and things function in the way that they do and is just as likely to be captivated by Sagittarius as any other zodiac sign.

Friendship brings a sort of joyful sharing and a common happiness in each other's company. Neither sign will find the other in any way tedious or boring and their general outlook on life is apt to be the same. Family relationships between these two should be warm and friendly, though not overly close.

When these individuals take the plunge and set up home together, a sort of frenetic refinement begins to develop as the driving, haphazard qualities of Sagittarius are contrasted with the ability of Aquarius to keep things looking and feeling good. Sagittarius can be very brash and brassy, but becomes less so when complemented by Aquarius, who definitely has more finesse. This does not mean that the Water Bearer is in any way staid or set in its ways.

Many couples from this sign combination find themselves living far from the shores of their birth, since both are great travellers and would love the challenge of a new culture. The Archer and the Aquarian are both extremely open-minded. Sagittarius may not find it too hard to be loyal to its Aquarian mate, who is capable of ringing the changes and keeping the Archer guessing.

Freshness is the hallmark of this pairing, together with the fact that Sagittarius never really knows what Aquarius is thinking, or even how it is likely to react next. This may well prove to be very important.

 ## SAGITTARIUS meets PISCES

Any neediness in this relationship generally comes from the direction of Pisces, which in almost any association with Sagittarius tends to rely on the Archer a good deal. However, this only really applies to social settings. Behind closed doors the situation could be very much reversed. This pairing may be distinctly 'odd' but it does have the capacity to work with a little effort on both sides.

Pisces is not generally the most self-confident zodiac sign and responds well to both flattery and encouragement. These it will get in abundance from Sagittarius, and particularly so in any sort of working environment. It is rare, however, to find the combination working well if Pisces is at the top of the tree, with the Archer lower down, but Sagittarius can be very adaptable so that even this is not out of the question.

Where a family attachment is concerned, Pisces is the party who always remembers to send that birthday card, with the Archer invariably forgetting and making a hasty telephone call at the last minute. Friends with this combination will have an unusual relationship – often quite close but difficult for others to fathom. There may be a deep mutual reliance that isn't immediately obvious.

Sagittarius and Pisces do not often form a romantic bond. If the relationship has already lasted any length of time, Pisces may have come to believe that to trust Sagittarius is to take the sort of chance that would make it nervous. Nevertheless it isn't out of the question because Pisces, a Water sign, often does set up home with Fire signs such as Sagittarius. However, it is important to realise that the Archer needs constant stimulus, which Pisces may sometimes find difficult to offer. Pisceans often have long, quiet periods, which unnerve Sagittarians and may drive them out to find the nearest party.

This is certainly a hard relationship for outsiders to understand and mutual friends may not be very common. Although not all romances depend upon individuals who have to share each and every moment and who cannot survive without each other, ideal Piscean matches are usually of this type.

Chapter 10
Capricorn
22 December to 20 January

 CAPRICORN meets ARIES

This seems a fairly odd combination. Aries is a go-getter, a no-nonsense success story on legs. Immediacy is all-important to the Ram, who will often use just about any method to achieve its objectives. All of this is in striking contrast to Capricorn, who is slow, steady and extremely hard-working. However, it may be the differences that cause this match to function well.

When faced with a common purpose such as work, Capricorn and Aries approach tasks in different ways but in most respects their strategies could prove to be very complementary. Aries functions well as a spokesperson and is the one to put forward startling ideas, while Capricorn works long and hard behind the scenes to put the plans into action. Capricorn is meticulous about detail and can turn Aries' dreams into hard and fast realities. The only problem may be whether it can achieve these objectives in the time-scales laid down by Aries.

Although deep, abiding friendships between the Goat and the Ram are not all that common, these too work rather well. Capricorn needs encouragement and probably looks at Aries with a sense of wonder but it certainly isn't intimidated, and despite its quiet ways it is a good intellectual match for the Ram.

In terms of deeper attachments, much will depend on the respective roles they adopt. Aries must believe that it rules the roost, even if this is not actually the case. The Ram does not tend to look deeply into attachments and is fairly superficial in its view of such matters. Despite its emotional depth, Capricorn also tends to be quite pragmatic at heart. It is unlikely therefore that this would be a 'hearts and flowers' type of union, though it might be immensely successful on a practical and financial level. Capricorn will be found at home more than Aries, who prefers to be out and about.

A word of warning for Aries: Capricorn can be incredibly stubborn at times. This alone might prove to be a significant stumbling-block.

CAPRICORN meets TAURUS

As friends and also as family members, Capricorn and Taurus usually function very well. It is only when we consider the deeper ramifications of a life spent together that things begin to 'creak' somewhat. At heart, however, there is much in common here since both signs respond to the Earth element and there is a natural understanding that should always prove comfortable, though perhaps not inspiring.

Capricorn and Taurus work together quite happily and very comfortably, particularly if they are involved in the same sort of tasks. Both signs know how to work hard and can do so for sustained periods, even if Taurus takes a little more 'getting going' than the Goat. Arguments between these two at any level will be very rare matters indeed, but so will inspiration and spontaneity. Rapid progress is therefore not to be expected in any situation in which Capricorn and Taurus meet. However, it must be said that the individuals concerned do not recognise this fact or even care about it.

Family ties with this combination should prove harmonious, with a notable lack of aggression or animosity of any kind.

Capricorn–Taurus is not a combination that commonly leads to deep attachments, perhaps because neither sign has the confidence to make the first approach. However, such relationships do exist and tend to be extremely steady affairs. The two have much in common, including a deep sense of love, with Taurus definitely leading in the romance stakes. Working towards shared objectives is not hard for this couple and there may well be a slow and steady climb towards aims that will find Capricorn and Taurus eventually achieving a great deal.

The only really important factor that has to be addressed is whether or not either of them actually feels stretched or enlivened by their life together. Both signs probably work best when allied in a romantic sense to more positive and dynamic zodiac types. When together, it is easy for both Capricorn and Taurus to become set in their ways, so in order to maintain interest both should use a good deal of imagination.

 ## CAPRICORN meets GEMINI

There is great scope within this pairing, and on just about any level. True, Capricorn and Gemini are radically different types of individuals but that should not prevent a great deal of very useful cross-fertilisation and an immediate liking that with the fullness of time can become very much more. In the case of Capricorn and Gemini it is hard to differentiate between the different sorts of relationship, since the same ground rules apply in each case. Capricorn is sometimes lacking in confidence and can gain this from a frequent association with those born under the sign of the Twins. Gemini is brash, communicative and outgoing, though with a very definite lack of self-confidence that can be bolstered by the very presence of the Goat. Ground rules are not hard to establish because the two signs function in different ways. It is unlikely that there will be frequent arguments in a situation like this, where there is a good deal of mutual respect. Capricorn has the ability to slow Gemini to a sensible speed, and the constant presence of Gemini will eventually force the Goat to at least a canter.

As lovers, Capricorn and Gemini can form a formidable partnership. They can't expect to hold everything in common – that would be far too much to ask – but in a way it is better that they don't, because it's the originality in each individual that contributes to overall success. At heart, Capricorn people are very funny, albeit in a dry way. Gemini appreciates this because it too has a startling and ready wit. Gemini also recognises and encourages the degree of intelligence that the Goat possesses and will always encourage it in social situations. Capricorn is not really a party animal but can put on a passable show when in the company of those born under the sign of the Twins. Together these two types form an entertaining attachment and one that is of significant interest to others. Friends will always be part of the scenario and may revel in their joint company.

Capricorn needs to allow Gemini some space for personal exploration, however.

CAPRICORN meets CANCER

Capricorn and Cancer are astrological opposites, which means the signs appear opposite each other in the zodiac wheel. Despite this, they have much in common and get on extremely well together. Both are 'cardinal' signs, which brings an instant understanding in certain respects, and although Capricorn and Cancer may have different objectives and don't always function in the same way, they do have an instinctive rapport.

When it comes to natural warmth, and an ability to display it, Cancer is the winner every time. However, this sign is also inclined to retreat. Capricorn, though not particularly progressive, does move forward, rolling slowly through the world at large. This makes Capricorn look solid when viewed by the Crab, which is happy to proceed slowly behind lumbering but irrepressible Capricorn.

Friendships between these signs are not dynamic affairs, but they personify loyalty and a common sense of fairness and decency. The same is true in working relationships, though the combination works best when neither individual is constantly forced into the public eye or put in a position where instant decisions are necessary.

As life partners, Capricorn and Cancer can achieve much by low-key discussion, followed by constant, steady action. Cancer is the more naturally romantic of the two, though even the Crab does need some encouragement. As a result, this pairing is hardly likely to demonstrate 'burning passion' and usually settles down into a situation of comfort and deep friendship. Since being good pals is halfway to conjugal bliss, there is little reason why Capricorn and Cancer together should not succeed in marriage.

The Crab loves to travel, whereas the Goat does not – which might prove to be a bone of contention. Both deal in the same way with home surroundings and family responsibilities. As a result, a sense of comfort and security certainly should not be lacking. What may be in somewhat short supply is a sense of excitement.

 CAPRICORN meets LEO

This is one of the most advantageous and interesting associations for Capricorn. True, the two zodiac signs function in entirely different ways, but this might be the very reason why the Goat and the Lion form such an interesting partnership at just about any level.

The Lion is an honourable type, an individual of great personal aspiration and considerable courage. These are qualities that the Goat respects tremendously. Capricorn can be enormously supportive, especially when it encounters someone that it instinctively likes and respects. As a result, we find both individuals in this combination offering the very best of what they are to support the other. There could hardly be a better platform than this for building any sort of relationship.

Many extremely successful business partnerships arise from the association of Capricorn and Leo. The Lion is a Fire sign, a go-getter, an individual who knows how to get things done, though not necessarily in a wholly practical sense. What it lacks in this respect Capricorn can offer in great measure and it does this willingly because it knows that Leo will share the ultimate success. It is not that Capricorn is in the least interested in the trappings of success, except in a material sense: it simply knows that Leo has to rule the pride. For itself, the Goat is determined, and just as strong in its own way as is Leo. Those born under the sign of the Lion realise this fact and can appreciate the positive qualities of Capricorn better than anyone.

As life partners, Capricorn and Leo can forge a union of great depth and happiness. Some of the Goat's darker qualities are counterbalanced by the natural light that shines from Leo's sunny nature. Leo doesn't specifically set out to change Capricorn, whom it already respects. All the same, there is a sort of process of change taking place here which is almost miraculous in some cases.

Leo can offer a sense of romance that Capricorn appreciates but finds somewhat more difficult to express.

 CAPRICORN meets VIRGO

Although this is a recipe for a fairly quiet and lacklustre sort of relationship, Capricorn and Virgo have one important factor in common: they are both Earth signs. This offers shared aspirations and a degree of understanding that ensures these people will come to like each other. Only the spark of genuine individuality may be missing from what is otherwise a promising attachment.

One of the best ways for Capricorn and Virgo to come together is through work. Virgo is more intuitive and exhibits a more nervous nature than Capricorn. The Goat offers solid, practical support and makes it possible for Virgo to be more confident. Virgo also likes to talk. It is fortunate therefore that Capricorn is an excellent listener and will rarely be bored with what Virgo has to say. They share common aims at almost every level, and this is just as obvious when these zodiac signs are joined in friendship as in a family tie. The mutual demands that each sign makes of the other are great, but generally exercised in areas that cause no real problems. At heart, Capricorn and Virgo understand each other – a good base for any association.

On a personal level, this relationship will tend to be a low-key affair. The earthiness of each partner can make for a good physical attachment, though romance in the strict sense of the word probably will not be present in great measure. Whilst this might be a problem to some people, deep down Capricorn and Virgo are both no-nonsense signs and will be happy with practical expressions of love.

These signs definitely do have what it takes to build a prosperous, tidy and mutually satisfying home. The inspiration for much of this will come from Virgo and be put into place by the more practical Capricorn. Excitement may be in short supply here and does need to be deliberately sought out. Travel may not be a natural choice for either sign, but is good for both and will bring a new dimension to the relationship.

Action is the key to greater contentment and will give Capricorn and Virgo more to talk about in the years that lie ahead. There is likely to be great staying-power in this match and few real disagreements.

CAPRICORN meets LIBRA

This is certainly not a bad pairing, although most of the effort in a social sense really does have to come from Capricorn. This fact remains true no matter what relationship the two individuals enjoy. Libra is extremely friendly and is good for Capricorn to have around – but the Goat has to put in that extra amount of effort to compensate for its own naturally quiet ways.

Although those born under the sign of the Goat are not the most outgoing and talkative people, they do respond well to being in the company of happy and interesting types. In this respect, Libra makes an ideal associate for Capricorn and offers a great deal of stimulation. The natural diplomacy of those born under the sign of the Scales means that they are not likely to test Capricorn's stubborn qualities, whilst their love of harmony also appeals to the Goat, who is not particularly interested in making too many waves.

As friends, Capricorn and Libra may be associated for many years. There's nothing too intense about the pairing and the friendship will not often deal in matters of earth-shattering importance.

In a family situation, the pairing is always good, with the more social qualities tending to come from Libra but plenty of input from Capricorn once it is prompted.

On a deeper and more personal level, this could prove to be a relationship that will strengthen and prosper with the passing of time. Capricorn is immensely practical, which Libra often is not. Libra feels somewhat protected by the solidity of Capricorn and responds by spending time lightening the load of the Goat, who can occasionally take itself and life a little too seriously. A good sense of humour is likely to develop. Libra responds to funny people and though Capricorn displays its humorous side in a fairly low-key way, Libra will react well.

The important message here is for Capricorn: keep it light and search for variety, because Libra, despite its sterling qualities, can so easily become bored. Travel is a must, as is an acquired ability for Capricorn to ring the changes both socially and on the domestic front.

 ## CAPRICORN meets SCORPIO

On the surface, this might not appear to be a particularly good match, though when the situation is analysed at a deeper level Capricorn and Scorpio people do have the potential to get along very well together. It's going to be a fairly quiet encounter but that doesn't matter since neither of these zodiac signs has any great need for excitement.

Scorpio is a very deep sign and quite difficult for many people to understand. It has levels of emotion that would be something of a mystery to all but the most perceptive type. To Capricorn this isn't really a problem because it's so inclined to take life in its stride. This ability to accept things as they are allows Capricorn to deal with qualities within Scorpio that can often be a problem to Scorpio itself as well as the world at large. Such is the equilibrium of the generally docile Capricorn nature that Scorpio generally remains calm and self-possessed when associated with it. Like all emotional types, the Scorpio reacts specifically to outside stimuli. Capricorn does not provoke or threaten this match, so that in simple friendship and close family ties, we have in this pairing two individuals who should have no problem hitting it off.

It may be difficult for these two ever to find themselves in a romantic clinch, simply because both are quite quiet. However, when it does happen the results can be extremely fortunate. Scorpio loves the practical and reliable Goat and probably understands what makes it tick as well as anyone ever could. Capricorn, meanwhile, gains much from the depths of feeling of which Scorpio is capable. It's true that this is not likely to be a particularly reactive match, socially speaking. Capricorn is low-key, but can be very physical and has strong endurance. At a deeply personal level, this can be an important factor because Scorpio's passion often takes on a physical manifestation.

The prognosis is good for practical success and there should be good earning and saving power when Capricorn and Scorpio come together. All that might sometimes be missing is a certain degree of excitement, though it is unlikely that either of these individuals would want or miss it.

 ## CAPRICORN meets SAGITTARIUS

There is a natural affinity here that often happens with two zodiac signs that are located next to each other in the zodiac wheel. At first, it may seem as if the two actually have very little in common in their basic natures, though this may turn out to be an advantage rather than a problem. The fact is that Capricorn and Sagittarius like each other, and there could hardly be a better starting-point than that.

Capricorn people are occasionally inclined to take themselves too seriously. That is difficult to do in the presence of Sagittarius, a sign that revels in action and a generally happy disposition. In almost any association, the Archer lightens the load of the Goat and helps it to recognise some of its own absurdity. This may be one of the most important factors in this match and shows at almost every level, from social to deeply personal.

It's likely that Capricorn and Sagittarius will work well together, keeping up a string of jokes, anecdotes and pleasantries on the way. Capricorn offers solidity that the Sagittarian is inclined to lack, also bringing a practicality to the relationship and an ability to put in the hours necessary to turn the Archer's schemes into reality.

It is quite common to find Capricorn and Sagittarius setting up home together. There is a natural co-reliance in this pairing that allows the Archer to live a more settled life. This probably turns out to be the case partly because Capricorn has stamina at every level, which is essential when irrepressible Sagittarius is part of the scenario. The Archer wants and actually desperately needs change and it might appear that this could become a stumbling-block because Capricorn is so often a stay-at-home sign. However, when in the company of Sagittarius, the Goat is far more likely to rouse itself to action and, once it does so, tends to enjoy the cut and thrust of life.

Sagittarius will always lead the pair socially, but when it comes to getting things done, Capricorn comes into its own to a greater degree. Common social contacts will be important but this is a pairing that naturally attracts friends.

A happy home and family life is likely here, producing children who will inherit a very balanced view of life.

CAPRICORN meets CAPRICORN

Rome wasn't built in a day, but if we are looking for a pair of individuals guaranteed to erect an entire city in the fullness of time, we could hardly do better than Capricorn and Capricorn Ltd. You won't even notice the presence of these individuals much of the time, except for the fact that their capacity for production and their practical common sense will cause more than a few surprises.

It is very satisfying for any Capricorn subject to know that they are allying their own nature to one that is bound to be very similar. True, the saying 'Too many cooks spoil the broth' could occasionally refer to the Capricorn assembly but this will rarely be the case. These are people who find it easy to second-guess each other and who can be relied upon to work efficiently and calmly together. When the rest of the world is falling apart, Capricorn and Capricorn have the ability to stroll in calmly and put everything right.

At the level of friendship, there is perhaps not much social chit-chat, though this should not prevent Capricorn people associating happily with each other. They tend to be quiet but they have a whole selection of common interests and a natural understanding that is worth much.

If it's a truly practical and well-ordered domestic life that counts, two Capricorns should be in seventh heaven, not that many people will get the chance to view the spectacle at first hand. One slightly difficult factor here is that, left to its own devices, Capricorn isn't the most social animal. It stands to reason therefore that two Capricorns together are not going to set the social world alight. These two really are the quiet couple next door who get on with their lives, rarely have parties and always keep their gardens tidy. Few people would find fault with the combination but neither would this be the first port of call when going first-footing on New Year's morn.

This is a relationship that simply works well and can go on doing so for many years.

CAPRICORN meets AQUARIUS

This is one of the zodiac relationships in which Capricorn has the chance truly to come into its own. Aquarius has everything necessary to bring out the best in the Goat, which offers a level of timely support that Aquarius does tend to relish. It's more social than the Capricorn–Capricorn pairing and can produce an entertaining double act that is immensely attractive to others.

Capricorn needs ideas. It is good at doing but it is especially successful when it is stimulated by outside influences. Unfortunately, it doesn't suffer fools gladly, so that there are a number of friendships and working relationships that it would tend to shun. A coming-together with Aquarius certainly isn't one of them. Aquarius offers Capricorn the chance to let its more zany side show and try new and different experiences and encounters. There is a definite indication of potential success when Capricorn and Aquarius ally their very different skills, together with an ability to entertain each other, and the world at large, on the way.

Family ties of this type are especially close.

There ought to be no difficulty in Capricorn and Aquarius getting together as life partners – they enjoy a natural liking that could easily turn into something much deeper. Aquarius is original and even odd at times, which the Goat finds refreshing and deals with easily. This is simply a case of zodiac magnetism, in which the sheer diversity of the two signs involved is part of the reason for the potential success.

Aquarius is less tidy than Capricorn. The domestic bliss the Goat enjoys with Aquarius means a degree of upheaval, and perhaps on occasions this might be a slight problem. On the whole, however, there is plenty to keep this relationship on track. Although finances may sometimes be precarious, thanks to Aquarius, Capricorn has an instinct for steering a sensible course.

In this and other ways, it prevents Aquarius from worrying as much as might sometimes be the case.

A happy union is likely here, together with good family instincts and the sort of humour that helps any union.

 ## CAPRICORN meets PISCES

The world doesn't get the opportunity to see Capricorn and Pisces interacting very often, except on those occasions when they are brought together by circumstances beyond their own control, for example work or family ties. The reason is simple – these two signs both respond better when faced with people who are more progressive than they are, so they tend not to team up in the first place.

There is a very friendly edge to this association, however. It would be hard to conceive of many circumstances in which Capricorn and Pisces would fall out. Pisces is so kind and attentive that it can get on with just about anyone, but it is also desperately deep and really difficult to understand fully and Capricorn may not be inclined to put in the necessary effort. The Goat is, after all, a fairly elusive animal itself. The saving grace in a work situation is that Capricorn applies itself in a very practical manner to almost anything. Pisces is not short of ideas and does tend to be more centred in its attitude when the Goat is around. This would be an excellent family association, though even here, out of choice, the two individuals may not spend a great deal of time together.

On a personal level, this seems to be one of the least likely unions. Neither Capricorn nor Pisces, if both signs are typical, will find it easy to pop the question. When it does happen, however, there is little to report that could be said to be genuinely negative. Perhaps the problem is that there would be little to report at all! Both of these zodiac signs respond well to stimulation from outside, but neither is particularly good at supplying it. There may be genuine and enduring love present in the match, and probably at a depth that few could fathom, but is that really enough in the end? This couple need the outside world and the things it can offer, by which I mean things that are not present in the relationship. As long as the gaze of both is directed outwards rather than inwards, there may be a chance of happiness. Certainly Pisces is deeply intuitive, a fact that would fascinate Capricorn.

On the whole, this is not a common match and it probably isn't too difficult to see why.

Chapter 11
Aquarius
21 January to 19 February

 AQUARIUS meets ARIES

This is an unusual sort of attachment, but because Aquarius is an Air sign, and so therefore very adaptable, there is a fair chance of it working on just about any level. Aries is a go-getter, whose greatest motivation in life is to achieve things. Reasons are irrelevant to the Ram – things are necessary and that is all. Nothing could be further from the truth in the case of Aquarius, who is much more inclined to ask 'Why?' For this reason alone, Aries will often find Aquarius too analytical, whilst Aquarius will consider the Ram to be lacking in subtlety and perhaps even a little coarse.

As friends, these individuals will keep up a lively debate about anything and everything. Aquarius can be the peacemaker but tends not to show such characteristics around Aries. More often than not, Aries will lose its temper with Aquarius's insistence that it is the 'method' that matters, something that is so often lost on the impetuous, driving, impatient Ram. The very reaction of the pairing may bring a tendency towards business success but it will be a turbulent ride because Aquarius is a 'fixed' sign and can be very stubborn.

Both zodiac signs are good travellers and, when together, can easily find themselves earning money more easily than when alone.

Family life is apt to be somewhat turbulent and disagreements are the rule rather than an exception. Despite this, a common respect can, ultimately, turn into an abiding love. In all probability, the level of mutual appreciation is there from the word go, whilst what the world views is simply the outward manifestation of what is happening deep inside.

Should Aquarius and Aries ever decide to tie the knot, the result would certainly be interesting and interactive. Despite the fact that these individuals will discuss and argue about practically every detail in life, it is possible for them to maintain a whole selection of friends who are held in common. The pairing sharpens the wits and intellects of both parties and the very existence of the relationship can enliven everyone and everything around them.

AQUARIUS meets TAURUS

Here we find an association that works extremely well on any level. Aquarius shows every ounce of its adaptability when paired up with easy-going and affable Taurus. It is true that both these signs are 'fixed', indicating that, given the right circumstances, both could prove to be extremely stubborn. In reality, this doesn't usually become an issue because Aquarius and Taurus are so busy enjoying each other's company, they don't seem to want to rub each other up the wrong way. There is a natural balance of forces when the Air-sign adaptability of Aquarius meets the refined, artistic and basically gentle Bull.

In a working association, the atmosphere will be lively and interesting with Aquarius and Taurus around. Disagreements ought to be kept to a minimum and mutual successes will be both frequent and well received. Some tendency to lack motivation is possible, though this could so easily spring from the fact that Aquarius and Taurus are so busy talking and having a good time, they don't apply themselves properly.

Friendship would almost certainly exist beyond the working environment. Both signs are basically sociable and the Bull even more so when Aquarius is around. There should be a common interest in the more 'refined' aspects of life and the décor of any location may be a common source of discussion. Aquarius and Taurus find it easy to enjoy mutual friends and to develop very similar interests.

Because of the genuine interest that these zodiac signs tend to have in each other, it is common to find them relishing a relationship that goes much deeper than ordinary friendship. However, it must be remembered that no matter how serious this attachment, it is because Aquarius and the Bull are such very good friends that the situation works as well as it does. Neither sign is especially competitive, but both want to please other people, and each other especially so.

Ardent and sincere, the Bull will move mountains for Aquarius, who, although in a more quirky way, will return the favour and do everything it can to show Taurus how important it is.

 # AQUARIUS meets GEMINI

This is a definite meeting of equals, with great potential and more than a modicum of excitement for both parties. Gemini is capricious, outgoing, happy and easy to please. Aquarius enjoys similar qualities, whilst at the same time managing to be even more quirky than Gemini. Both individuals are born under Air signs, which means they are natural communicators. At the same time there is enough basic difference in the two natures to create a cross-fertilisation of interest that will keep both Aquarius and Gemini busy for any length of time.

When together, Aquarius and Gemini frequently put on a double act that positively demands an audience, and playing to the gallery comes as second nature to both parties. Aquarius may be somewhat quieter than Gemini, but certainly not much, and it will never be overpowered by anyone. These individuals work well together and bring a breath of fresh air and a new approach to almost anything they address.

Family ties between these two come about very often and usually promote a harmonious, if somewhat reactive, attachment. Gemini and Aquarius are both natural party animals and age doesn't matter when it comes to the magnetism that passes between them.

Great scope exists here for a long and happy personal attachment. True, it will often seem unusual when viewed through the eyes of others, but the very originality of the pairing is what gives it zest and potential staying-power. There will be a few tiffs, if only because Aquarius and Gemini both want to rule the roost. Such power struggles are more or less inevitable but are hardly likely to lead to any serious or long-term disagreements. In this pair, we have people who share a common desire to have fun, but who both seek to expand their knowledge of the world and its infinite diversity.

The signs of Aquarius and Gemini breed people of above-average intelligence and this would be a relationship that exists as much on a mental level as anywhere else. Advantages come through quick-thinking, travel and a generally good potential for sharing.

 ## AQUARIUS meets CANCER

Aquarius is motivated by a basic need to know. Cancer is very different and 'feels' its way through life. The Crab is an emotional creature in zodiac terms and shows this tendency in almost everything it does. However, these facts should not be taken as indicators that this relationship will be anything less than cordial or generally successful. On the contrary, it might be suggested that Cancer makes one of the best friends and general allies that Aquarius is ever likely to encounter. It is extremely unusual to find these zodiac signs at odds with each other.

Naturally retiring and very sensitive, Cancer responds extremely well to the happy-go-lucky and instinctive approach to life that is second nature to the Water Bearer. Aquarius gains too, simply because Cancer, at any level of association, can offer a degree of depth that Aquarius alone often lacks. Actually this may not be the case at all and those born under the sign of the

Crab have an innate ability to find depths within Aquarius that it might not even realise it possesses. Outright success in working partnerships shouldn't be in doubt, though something of the 'edge' associated with Aquarius when in the company of more positive zodiac signs is apt to be missing in this case.

As mutual family members, Aquarius and Cancer create a particularly harmonious environment. Cancer is especially fond of other family members, and none more so than Aquarius.

It is the basic difference between these two zodiac signs that brings about their tendency towards success at any level, but especially when there is a personal attachment present. Cancer is a homemaker and, whether it realises the fact or not, Aquarius needs to feel secure. When the Crab offers so much practical support, much of which is behind the scenes, Aquarius can easily carry on with its search for the meaning of life. Both parties, therefore, get pretty much what they want from this pairing and the reasons for the happiness that is created are not especially profound. Cancer loves to be loved, and Aquarius, when with Cancer, does not find it at all hard to be faithful, concerned and very protective.

 ## AQUARIUS meets LEO

There is much that is both stimulating and mutually satisfying about this combination, which is likely to be something of a winner from the very beginning. Aquarius, being naturally inquisitive, is instinctively attractive to Leo. Although those born under the zodiac sign of the Lion are somewhat more regal and even overbearing than the average Aquarian, this need not be too much of a problem. Aquarius is adaptable – perhaps the most adaptable zodiac sign of them all. It looks at Leo with the same interest it shows in all the people it meets, though the natural attachment here is likely to be greater than Aquarius engenders in most cases.

This is a particularly good attachment when seen from the point of view of co-operation, which should ensure that Aquarius and Leo make good workmates. Aquarius is interested in the overall patterns of life, whilst Leo is better able to concentrate on specific tasks. The Lion relishes the inherent refinement of Aquarius and although it can sometimes find difficulties dealing with the classless quality of Aquarius, it respects the fact that it is allied to a zodiac sign that finds little difficulty getting on with anyone. The fact is that Leo can be quite pompous on occasions. Aquarius, fortunately, finds this amusing, rather than annoying. There is a good deal of gentle teasing going on here, and much of it comes from Aquarius. Leo is intelligent enough to realise the fact and responds cheerfully and with very good humour.

When allied together in marriage or a long-term relationship, Aquarius and Leo are hardly likely to be bored. There is always a great deal to talk about and the two ought to enjoy a happy and reactive home life. The Aquarian form of love is less noble than that of Leo but these two zodiac signs are willing to learn from experience and can gain markedly from long periods in each other's company.

Leo's basic nature does not have the same curiosity that is meat and drink to Aquarius, but both zodiac signs tend to produce basically intelligent individuals who are bound to learn much from each other.

 ## AQUARIUS meets VIRGO

Although not a bad pairing, there are inherent difficulties in this relationship, unless both parties put in a degree of extra effort. There are fundamental differences in the ways Aquarius and Virgo think about life and sometimes, and in almost any sort of association, these differences bubble to the surface and bring friction that will cause Aquarius to retreat – not because it is intimidated, but rather because it is bored. Virgo doesn't altogether understand what makes the Water Bearer tick, though both signs are basically garrulous and should be able to quite easily talk their way through situations that could otherwise turn out to be a problem.

Aquarius has a tendency to act on impulse. This is much less likely with Virgo, who may sometimes wonder at the ability of Aquarius to think on its feet to the extent that it does. Everything is neat and tidy in the world of Virgo, even if this is not always apparent. Meanwhile, the Aquarian mind is like a badly wound ball of wool, from which loose threads emerge in every possible direction. Virgo is intuitive enough to recognise this and wants to smooth out the irregularities in the Aquarian nature – a definite mistake. Disagreements and sometimes outright arguments can result from clashes of will, which generally stem from simple misunderstandings.

Family relationships may also be occasionally contentious and if it comes to a dispute, Virgo can certainly teach Aquarius a thing or two about sulking.

This combination doesn't provide the most common form of romantic attachment, but it is not by any means impossible. The important thing to note is that both these signs have to learn to compromise. Much adaptation must come from Aquarius, who has the facility to compartmentalise its life. In other words, Aquarius will behave differently towards Virgo from the way it displays itself to other zodiac types. This can be something of a mystery to Virgo, who maintains its basic nature throughout.

It has to be said that there is not an instinctive meeting of minds here but this, in itself, could promote a mutual interest that could last for years.

AQUARIUS meets LIBRA

This is generally a happy and productive pairing. Because both Aquarius and Libra are Air signs, there is already a common understanding that manifests itself at almost every level. Libra is diplomatic and more than able to cope with the sometimes erratic and strange world of the Aquarian. Rather than finding Aquarius difficult to deal with, Libra absolutely relishes what those born under the Water Bearer have to bring to the party. There are mutual gains through communication and mental motivation and even the likelihood of a sort of intuitive understanding when these signs meet.

In the main, Libra and Aquarius do things in more or less the same way. This has to be an advantage, if only because it means there will be no constant checking and rechecking of information within this association. For this reason alone, the two signs tend to work well together. They can be productive and even very successful when the motivation is right. As partners in some self-employed venture, Aquarius and Libra can be second to none and arguments between them will be very rare indeed.

Friendship brings a meeting of minds and almost certainly common interests because both Aquarius and Libra are enthusiastic about life in all its diversity. Aquarius may be the quieter one – though only just.

Aquarius and Libra can make one of the best personal matches, which allows both parties a degree of liberty, allied to a sense of common purpose. Any Air-sign individual is likely to wander in a relationship that it finds to be stifling but when two come together, as in this case, the desire to explore other attachments at a deep level is likely to be less intense. Aquarius gradually offers Libra more confidence and convinces it to show a more assertive side, whilst Libra is on hand when Aquarius needs a better sense of balance and, perhaps, a slightly more rational view of the world at large. A deep and abiding love may well develop, with great interdependence.

 ## AQUARIUS meets SCORPIO

There isn't anything particularly ordinary about this association at any level. The two zodiac signs here are motivated in entirely different ways and one might be left with the impression that they have little or nothing in common. Actually Aquarius and Scorpio generally tend to get on fairly well. They both have a sense of fascination with the extraordinary – and this category includes the attachment they share. This is undoubtedly a weird union and yet it proves to be attractive, not only for the parties concerned but also for the world at large.

Aquarius tends to 'adopt' Scorpio, at least in situations such as work. Scorpio is quiet and those born under the zodiac sign of the Water Bearer generally assume that quiet people are somehow unhappy. Of course this isn't the case, though the rather unorthodox qualities of Aquarius are attractive to Scorpio, who will co-operate as a result. Aquarius tends to be mystified by the silent power of the Scorpion and will dig and delve to try and nudge the real person to the surface. Of course it never happens and this fact alone means that Aquarius will spend a great deal of time studying Scorpio, rarely running out of steam and always willing to offer a helping hand on the way. Does Scorpio worry about the nature of the association? Not a bit. It is a reserved sign, but deeply intuitive. The mere fact that Aquarius is so odd is of extreme interest to Scorpio. As a result, any association offers both parties a degree of fascination.

As lovers, Aquarius and Scorpio find common ground in a home that is off-beat, though welcoming to outsiders. The Water Bearer is the naturally gregarious host, but Scorpio is a quick learner, and because it tends to feel content with Aquarius, Scorpio itself will begin to show a more friendly face to the world at large. This can be an intensely physical relationship and one that goes much deeper than the superficial mental attachments that Aquarius sometimes forges. Scorpio is very committed to home and family, whilst Aquarius loves to travel.

This is a relationship in which compromise prevails.

 ## AQUARIUS meets SAGITTARIUS

The fiery, changeable and sometimes capricious zodiac sign of Sagittarius may indeed meet its match when allied in any sort of attachment to Aquarius. It has to be pointed out from the start that there is nothing especially deep here. Both signs are mentally motivated and have an ability to analyse, though this quality goes much deeper in the case of Aquarius, who is quite likely to take Sagittarius to pieces intellectually. It does this with all signs, simply because it has an insatiable curiosity about the world and the people who live within it.

As partners in business, Aquarius and Sagittarius stand a much better than average chance of being successful. Each has what it takes to support the other at both a mental and a practical level. Both signs also enjoy having fun, so life won't be all work and no play. Any sort of mutual career that involves staying in contact with the world beyond the office or factory door will be a good choice and the co-operation at work is most likely in this case to extend to social matters.

As friends, Aquarius and Sagittarius are mutually supportive but neither is inclined to take life very seriously and since there is a good deal of interplay taking place on a mental level, this is a relationship that tends to attract others too. Concentrating on the task in hand isn't especially easy for either of these zodiac signs but somehow, when together, this becomes easier.

There are qualities about both signs that could easily lead to a common desire to travel. It isn't at all extraordinary to find Aquarius and Sagittarius moving around the world together, often finally settling in some location far from their common point of origin.

On a romantic level, there is going to be reaction here. Aquarius and Sagittarius can't expect to agree about everything. Clear lines of demarcation regarding the running of a household are essential, that is if either party is at home very much of the time. This is a mentally motivated relationship and one in which the tendency of both signs to be unfaithful may be catered for.

Aquarius keeps Sagittarius guessing and can easily assume different personas. This is usually a happy match.

AQUARIUS meets CAPRICORN

When the Water Bearer finds itself in the company of Capricorn, the union will be a profound one that responds very positively to the practical qualities that the Goat brings to all aspects of its life. There is an instant understanding that each of these zodiac signs has certain skills. They are unlikely to stand on each other's toes and will be willing to offer a sort of mutual support that can be useful at just about any level.

Capricorn loves to do things. It isn't fast in its approach to situations, though it does admire the sometimes lightning-quick deductions that Aquarius makes. In a work setting, Aquarius will often take the lead, leaving Capricorn to a supporting role, which it tends to enjoy better than being directly involved with the world, face to face. Mutual aims and objectives are possible, though not particularly necessary. It's the essential cross-referencing that matters in this association because, at heart, both signs are quite curious. The Goat will never fully understand what makes Aquarius function in the way that it does, but it remains fascinated and can't stop looking. Meanwhile, Aquarius always has something interesting to talk about and can show Capricorn a different sort of world.

In terms of living a happy and contented home life – and enjoying a physical and mental association that suits it well – Aquarius can do much worse than ally itself to Capricorn. There can be a great deal of teasing going on because Aquarius, itself a very funny sign, brings out the dry wit of Capricorn.

Whether Aquarius can find the degree of mental stimulation that it needs when living exclusively with the Goat may be in doubt. It is for this reason that the company of others is frequently sought. The couple are likely to have many friends, some mutual, some exclusive.

Family ties remain strong and raising children won't be difficult for this pair.

Aquarius and Capricorn can love deeply, though in a rather detached sort of way that outsiders might find difficult to fathom.

 ## AQUARIUS meets AQUARIUS

This is potentially one of the oddest and yet the most attractive relationships in the whole of the zodiac. This is because two Aquarians, when they come together, bring out the strangest, funniest and most endearing qualities inherent within the sign. Neither individual will actually seek to offer this very strange sort of union to the world at large – they simply can't help themselves. What follows is almost like a stage play, though definitely one that any audience would wish to see again and again.

Any alliance between Aquarius and Aquarius is going to be off-beat and odd. Despite this fact, and particularly when working side by side, Aquarians can get a great deal done. Friendly, generally superficial with each other, and always keen to attract the attention of the world at large, Aquarius and Aquarius work on steadily towards their objectives at one level, whilst enjoying a knockabout association that seems custom-built to please everyone. What goes on below the surface is a slightly different matter and probably remains within the realms of the mysterious. Aquarius only shows what it wishes to the world at large, and two Aquarians together form an alliance that is virtually impossible to analyse. Sparks that fly from this coming-together are like lightning – and it's difficult to know where the next bolt is going to strike.

Do these individuals have what it takes to live a long and contented personal life together? As with everything else associated with Aquarius and Aquarius, the answer is almost impossible to find. Aquarius is self-possessed and yet sociable. It is curious about the world at large, yet it can sometimes be practically inept. Two Aquarians together certainly means there will be plenty of entertainment, though whether anything would actually get done around the house remains to be seen.

At the end of the day, this romance is either going to work extremely well, or it won't function at all. At least Aquarius does have flexibility – a commodity that it is going to need in great measure when living in a situation that must be like constantly looking in a strange and distorted mirror.

AQUARIUS meets PISCES

Air signs, such as Aquarius, and Water signs, personified by Pisces, often seem to find common ground but this won't actually be the truth of the situation. Generally speaking, it isn't looking at life in the same way that makes people get on well – it is, rather, the fact that they each bring a different slant on life that makes it interesting. That's certainly what happens when Aquarius and Pisces come together.

Pisces can be shy, certainly introspective, and difficult to understand. As far as Aquarius is concerned that's fine, because the Water Bearer likes nothing better than to analyse, which it will be doing for ever in the case of Pisces. In any sort of relationship, Aquarius quite naturally takes the lead when it comes to contacts with the world at large, whilst Pisces is happiest in a supporting role and doesn't generally display an executive ability, even though it quite definitely could if it were so inclined.

Aquarius and Pisces can be very good friends and there will be a sense of refinement and culture in their relationships. This is not, for example, the sort of attachment that would find its best expression on a football terrace. Neither sign is especially noisy and Pisces needs to make an effort to show its more sociable and chatty side to Aquarius, who can easily grow bored if it doesn't seem to be making any sort of overall impression.

Family ties between these zodiac signs are strong and romantic ties should also stand the test of time. It really depends on the individuals concerned but as long as the Piscean half of the attachment is willing to work hard to keep Aquarius amused and diverted, all will be well. Although quieter than its Air-sign cousins, Aquarius does need the cut and thrust of social interplay in order to remain happy over weeks, months or years, whereas Pisces may not. Arguments will be few and far between – in fact they may never happen at all. It could be that the essential 'bite' is missing from this attachment and both zodiac signs will have to work hard to ensure that it was present at some level.

Aquarius and Pisces may enjoy a very peculiar sort of physical relationship but it suits them.

Chapter 12
Pisces
20 February to 20 March

 PISCES meets ARIES

We may see this as being an unlikely sort of attachment, though it does tend to work well, particularly at the deeply personal level. There are a number of reasons why this is so, the most important of which lies in what these very different zodiac signs have to offer each other. So radically opposed are Pisces and Aries in the way that they view the world, there is no threat from either side, a fact that is of particular significance to Aries in this attachment. Pisceans are very sensitive. It is not at all extraordinary to find those who are born under the zodiac sign of the Fishes dedicating practically their whole lives to a particular cause or person. At the same time, they are basically lacking in self-confidence and often think that the far more dynamic Aries individual can make them feel secure, particularly in practical matters.

As simple friends, common interests here are few, particularly since Pisces, though sociable, tends to opt for a generally quiet sort of life, which Aries definitely does not. In a work setting, however, the match works better. Pisces offers strong support and may well find that the average Aries personifies what Pisces would wish to be itself. Those born under the sign of the Fishes will readily take instructions from Aries but also have the ability to modify dramatically the thought processes and actions of the Ram.

It is at the level of romance and long-term relationships that this matching is most common. Aries individuals are naturally protective, which suits sometimes timid Pisces. This may not appear to be a coming-together of equals, though in the end even this may turn out to be the case. Aries is not half so sure of itself as it appears. The quiet yet wise support of Pisces is very welcome to the brash, impulsive Ram, which can show an extremely gentle side to its nature when Pisces is around.

Common ground will develop, even if each may retain its unique qualities. Any household formed by this pair will be secure, well run and happy.

PISCES meets TAURUS

This is a profound relationship. Pisces is probably the most difficult sign of the zodiac to understand, whilst Taurus, though more approachable and less complicated, can itself be quite difficult to fathom at times. The difficulty, if there is one, arises because Pisces finds it difficult to offer Taurus any tangible clue as to what its motivations and ideas may be. Taurus, being an Earth sign, is ruled by Venus and so can be quite lazy at times. So, on any relationship level, the Bull may not care to attempt to plumb the depths of the Piscean pool, which may bring about a potential problem.

There is hardly likely to be much animosity generated in this coming-together, so Pisces and Taurus can both work and live together in harmony. They each exhibit a great deal of kindness and understanding and may develop a lifelong attachment of sorts. A mutual respect is likely, as is the ability to build common objectives. What may be missing is that certain 'something' that comes from rubbing up against a character who is radically different. If both these individuals are typical of the zodiac signs into which they were born, the prognosis for a kind of contentment is good but much of what makes both Taurus and Pisces feel fulfilled could be missing. These facts may only be registered as a sort of subconscious 'emptiness' and, in some cases, will be dismissed almost instantly.

Romantically, Pisces and Taurus make for a very sympathetic liaison. Seen from the outside, these individuals may be viewed as kind and loving, with a distinctly demonstrative quality, particularly in the case of Pisces. Financial success may be possible, mainly thanks to Taurus, and the pair will gain greatly from an ability to search out new horizons whenever possible. A staid and steady life will be preferred but that can lead to a certain degree of avoidable tedium. Routines should therefore be shunned wherever possible, especially in the long term. A change is as good as a rest and particularly so when Taurus and Pisces come together. Pisces is very adaptable, which in the end could easily be the saving grace here.

 ## PISCES meets GEMINI

When a Water sign, such as Pisces, gets together with an Air sign, typified by Gemini, the prognosis is quite good. Certainly there can be an understanding that develops quickly, together with an instinctive liking that these signs acquire very early on. Both zodiac signs are 'dual' signs – there are two fish in the sign of Pisces, and Gemini, obviously, is a pair of twins – and though in some relationships this is a problem, it is less likely to be so in this case. Each sign has something to bring to the party and in the end it's this fact that counts the most.

Pisces is basically lacking in self-confidence, and also in motivation. Gemini, meanwhile, is all 'front' and appears to be the most 'together' person imaginable. Actually, nothing could be further from the truth, which is why the gentle support and encouragement offered by Pisces can be so important.

As friends, these individuals may not appear to have much in common. Gemini wants to be out there in the world, interacting with everyone and making a good impression, unlike the more retiring Pisces. However, because the sign of the Twins offers the necessary protection, Pisces may well be willing to take the plunge too. This will lead to a more positive Piscean individual beginning to develop and turns out to be one of the main reasons why the attachment can work.

As co-workers, Pisces and Gemini know well how to co-operate and as long as things are light-hearted there is also likely to be some success formed from this pairing.

Probably the best association for this couple lies in a long-lasting personal relationship. There is much more to the sign of the Fishes than at first meets the eye. Like all Air signs, Gemini is curious and longs to understand its Piscean mate. While it is probing away, Pisces is aware that it is being scrutinised, though even this sort of attention is welcome, the more so because Pisces recognises a great deal of kindness in Gemini and encourages it. The attitudes of the individuals involved in this romance can be very different but both are more than willing to give ground and discover a common way of viewing life that is comfortable for all concerned.

Pisces and Gemini make loving parents, and children born of this union should feel secure.

 ## PISCES meets CANCER

From the outset it has to be suggested that this is a pairing that probably works better at a superficial or family level than it would romantically. Pisces and Cancer will hardly ever find reason to fall out with each other. How could they? Both are motivated by the same basic desires and each is an extremely emotional zodiac sign. They share compassion, a deep social conscience and a desire to nurture. Neither sign is particularly gritty or reactive.

All of this contributes to a good potential for friendship, or else working towards common objectives in a family sense. Both signs can rise slowly and steadily to positions of some authority and each will respect the position and thought processes of the other.

Having said all that, Pisces and Cancer both work at their best when there is something to push against. Each is a Water sign, and the trouble is that water, despite its awesome power, does not know what to do when confronted by another body of water, which offers no resistance but simply retreats when pushed. The analogy works especially well when the two signs form a lifelong pact – which can so easily happen between people who seem to have so much in common. Life will be fairly easy-going, with little in the way of disruption and arguments, and a sense of purpose that is held very much in common. What may be lacking is the sort of excitement that makes both these zodiac signs feel more fulfilled. Either could take the lead under different circumstances but taking a chance is not that likely and as a result life could sometimes appear to be quite tedious.

Much energy will be committed towards home and family, however. A comfortable atmosphere is necessary for both the Crab and the sign of the Fishes and this is not difficult for the combination to achieve.

Pisces and Cancer can seem to be blissfully happy, but if the observer plumbs the subconscious depths of this pairing they will come to realise that things are not quite as simple as they first appear. Attention needs to be given to stretching the horizons of a world that could become just too comfortable when Pisces and Cancer are together. Deliberately setting new boundaries will offer incentives that both these signs need at heart.

 ## PISCES meets LEO

This is a relationship that generally works best when Leo considers itself to be the dominant sign, a state of affairs that Pisces doesn't seem to worry about too much. The only time Pisces and Leo fail to get on well is if the situation is reversed. Pisces can easily support Leo, but it cannot lead it by the hand. From an emotional point of view, it is very difficult for Leo ever to envisage a situation when it would fail to cherish and nurture Pisces, which it sees as vulnerable. The Leo ego is large, but easily dented. Pisces usually knows this fact and reacts accordingly. Pisces and Leo come together readily, and under many different circumstances.

Where work is concerned, this pair can function extremely well together. Invariably Leo will set the pace, with Pisces offering a good deal of support and slowing down the sometimes too impetuous ways of the Lion. Even at this level Pisces can be the power behind the throne, though of course it will never allow Leo to realise that such is the case and will always find ways to massage the Leo ego. Pisces is a wise zodiac sign, and in its own way perhaps the most powerful of them all. It is unlikely to be as materialistic as Leo, so overall success in any venture is viewed by the two signs in different ways.

As friends, Pisces and Leo are mutually supportive, though this sort of relationship is not as common as the much deeper attachment that often works so well.

Pisces loves to be loved and Leo knows how to offer the cheerful affection and protection that is so important to the sign of the Fishes. Leo itself is rarely as confident as it appears to be and can suffer from great doubts. Pisces is always on hand to offer timely advice, though without ever being any kind of threat to Leo's vanity. This is a romance in which everyone seems to gain, including the many mutual friends that this couple will make. Look out for a very happy home life, with a good sharing of responsibilities.

 ## PISCES meets VIRGO

This is not a particularly easy match to understand, or in which to be involved. The problem may come more from Pisces than from Virgo. The sign of the Virgin is naturally inquisitive and will be fascinated by a zodiac sign as deep and difficult to penetrate as Pisces can be. Nevertheless, the latent kindness of Pisces is obvious to all, including Virgoans, who revel in the sort of attention that can come their way from those born under the sign of the Fishes. There will be a certain quiet dignity in any version of this pairing, even if raw excitement is unlikely to be part of the communion. Perhaps this doesn't matter too much because both zodiac signs can be happy with their own company and, when together, they don't make too many waves.

Virgo and Pisces don't make the best working partners. It isn't that either zodiac sign is lazy or in any way unable to cope with the demands of work. A more likely explanation for any shortfall is that there simply isn't enough reaction going on. Any object that needs to move requires something to push against. When Virgo and Pisces come together, the point of resistance isn't immediately obvious. This can cause frustrations, more likely for Virgo than for the sign of the Fishes. Virgo doesn't always understand what Pisces is thinking, which can be infuriating to one whose whole nature is so inquisitive. In order to compensate for this, Pisces needs to make an extra effort to explain itself, its thoughts and motivations.

From the Piscean perspective, any romantic attachment with Virgo will be a quiet affair. Strangely enough it is at the level of an affair that the pairing may work best, for at least here there would be a degree of excitement. In a more orthodox romance, there must be 'happenings', engendered by both parties, though specifically by Pisces. Virgo is basically lacking in confidence. Pisces can offer this but it may tend to get rather tedious when Virgo swallows up everything the sign of the Fishes can provide and appears to give little in return.

Effort is needed in this attachment.

PISCES meets LIBRA

This ought to be a fortunate attachment at any level, if only because both Pisceans and Librans are such pleasant people. There is a distinct lack of 'edge' here and a willingness to share that make these two of the nicest people – especially when together. Pisces and Libra enjoy a natural rapport and extend the qualities they share so that the sum of the whole is greater than the parts.

Pisces has great sensitivity. This means that it tends to ally itself either with individuals who are entirely different by nature, or with those it recognises as being similar to itself. This is the essence of the Pisces–Libra tie. All the same, there are differences between the two zodiac signs. Libra tends to be more noisy and sociable, which is helpful when it comes to getting Pisces up to speed. Those born under the sign of the Scales can also be a great deal more fickle than the standard Piscean but that only makes Pisces more determined to show its own diverse qualities to the world at large.

A working relationship proves to be no problem at all, whilst family ties from these zodiac signs are usually happy and generally trouble-free.

As long as neither sign has previously experienced a bigger, brighter and more dynamic attachment, their common efforts in romance are apt to be very good. True, this isn't the most dynamic pairing that one is ever likely to behold but it carries a sort of quiet charisma that emanates from both parties. Libra is always ready for fun, as indeed is Pisces when it feels confident. The Scales have what it takes to bring Pisces out of itself and to ensure that the full scope of the sign is put on display. Pisces should beware, however: Libra needs excitement to a greater extent and so a settled, stay-at-home sort of life probably won't always be enough. Still, the world loves Pisces and Libra when they are together, which is no real surprise.

Common objectives here tend to revolve around family and also extend to building a beautiful home. Pisces has the ability to elevate the naturally intuitive qualities that Libra also possesses.

 ## PISCES meets SCORPIO

Here we have a couple who definitely do bring out the best in each other. From the word go it should be obvious that Pisces and Scorpio, when together, simply have a sort of magnetism that is extremely attractive to outsiders. Both are Water signs and that means there is a great deal of sensitivity in this pairing, though it doesn't indicate that there is any lack of 'bite', for in any attachments, from simple friendship to lifelong lover, Scorpio will defend Pisces tenaciously.

It is quite common to find Pisceans and Scorpio people enjoying a very happy friendship. The reasons are many. Scorpio has more 'oomph' than Pisces but tends to rely heavily on the intuitive qualities that those born under the sign of the Fishes possess.

When working together, Pisces and Scorpio can quietly achieve a great deal. Neither sign tends to spawn go-getters, so we shouldn't expect this pair to break records at any level. Scorpio is sometimes accused of being sarcastic and even a little cruel to others, but this side of the Scorpion rarely shows when Pisces is in attendance.

Family ties with multiple Water-sign personalities are extremely common and this is a match that leads to mutual support and domestic harmony.

When Pisces and Scorpio embark on a romantic attachment, they may be accused of being a little too locked into each other. It is all too easy for these people to retire into their own little castle and to shut out the world. When Scorpio discovers what it wants from a relationship, it loves with a passion that few other signs of the zodiac are able to understand – and fortunately Pisces can. It is unlikely that Pisces will feel stifled or intimidated by the sheer power that Scorpio finds in this union and the strangest thing of all is that this deep, abiding love will hardly be suspected by the world at large. Both Pisces and Scorpio know how to keep a secret and the best secret of all is just how close they can be.

This is a match that rarely fails and one that almost inevitably leads to a happy family life. Pisces is allowed to shine here, though it probably won't be 'stretched', which is a shame.

 ## PISCES meets SAGITTARIUS

Pisces is sensitive, deep and difficult to understand. Sagittarius, meanwhile, is outgoing, often accused of being shallow and not particularly inclined to spend long hours wondering what makes other people tick. As a result, Pisces might prove just a little too complicated for the Archer to try and assess in any detail.

Pisces and Sagittarius are often found teaming up as friends. Paradoxically, because Sagittarius generally moves on quickly from one pal to another, this is a friendship that could easily stand the test of time. Under these circumstances, Sagittarius gradually gets to know and like what it sees in Pisces, whilst those born under the sign of the Fishes are naturally inclined to look for and respect the protecting arm of a Fire sign such as the Archer. As co-workers, these signs also get on well, though generally better when Sagittarius is at the top of the tree, with Pisces on a slightly lower rung.

In family relationships, these types help to create interest and a strong social trend, allied to a sense of humour that is engendered by Sagittarius and perpetuated by Pisces.

When things get to a deeper, romantic level, slight problems can emerge. Sagittarius is ambitious and a person who likes to live the high life. Although Pisces will do its best to keep up it is, at heart, more of a home-bird than the Archer is ever likely to be. Another slight difficulty might arise in terms of mutual friends – or rather the lack of them. The ultimate success of this pairing really depends on Sagittarius, which isn't the most constant zodiac sign. Pisces is steadfast and can gradually convince the Archer that it couldn't get a better deal anywhere else.

It takes a great deal of patience to live happily for any length of time with a Sagittarian. Pisces has patience in abundance, so things could work out well in the end, despite some potential pitfalls. On those occasions when it does, Sagittarius learns a great deal about true passion.

 ## PISCES meets CAPRICORN

It is hard to imagine Pisces and Capricorn people falling out very often – both signs will work towards a peaceful life whenever possible. The problem is that with Pisces and Capricorn in the same relationship, life can be so peaceful that practically nothing happens at all. Despite the fact that both these zodiac signs can be quite progressive and successful when mixing with other zodiac types, they don't generally have what it takes to bring out the best in each other.

An exception might be a professional association, where Pisces and Capricorn are likely to get on extremely well. Capricorn is very practical and will work long and hard to achieve any number of objectives. Pisces can be hardworking too, and especially so if it understands that there is a sensible and rational objective to its efforts. Pisces is capable of being timid and in any relationship with Capricorn, it is the Goat that makes the running. This can be somewhat uncomfortable for Capricorn, who is happier when others are pushed to the front.

Can Pisces and Capricorn form a workable and happy romantic attachment? Of course it is possible, but it is sometimes doubtful whether what each of the parties concerned gets out of the romance is exactly what they would wish. Arguments will probably happen rarely, if at all. With time, a great deal of affection can be seen passing in both directions, though what may be missing is reaction, spark and just plain 'oomph'. The great outdoors will probably appeal to both these signs and a country life will suit them best.

Pisces and Capricorn together often positively court adversity, through either living or working circumstances, a strategy that will offer more in the way of struggle and perhaps some excitement on the way. Finances are generally settled for this pairing and there will be little to worry about in material terms. There is the potential for great physicality in this romance, though the world at large would never guess. However, neither sign is likely to act on impulse and that decreases excitement.

 ## PISCES meets AQUARIUS

Generally speaking, Water signs, such as Pisces, tend to get on well with those born under Air signs, of which Aquarius is an example. For this reason, Pisces readily teams up with Aquarius on a number of levels. It is hard to judge exactly how much success would be achieved if simple friendship passed to something much deeper, but it certainly isn't out of the question.

Pisces naturally likes Aquarius and is particularly drawn to its great kindness and depth, whilst at the same time revelling in its ready communication and its links with the world at large. Those born under the sign of the Fishes tend to be naturally refined and don't particularly like getting their hands dirty. Aquarius is very similar in this regard, although it may be rather more physical than Pisces.

In social situations, Pisces and Aquarius tend to get on extremely well. They have enough common interests to give rise to some entertaining conversations, and other people will be invited to join in too. At work, Pisces and Aquarius can function well side by side, though they may be at odds if Pisces has a position of greater authority. In matters of finance, Aquarius wants to rule the roost but the relationship will function better if it can learn to defer to Pisces.

At a deeper level, it has to be said that this relationship looks very different from the outside from the way it actually functions behind closed doors. Being an Air sign, Aquarius is supposed to be quite mentally motivated but it has deep physical depths that only a sign such as Pisces can truly understand. Aquarius will remain fascinated for years, attempting to fathom out what really makes Pisces tick, since those born under the sign of the Water Bearer have the greatest curiosity imaginable. With an interest in similar subjects and a capacity to form a deep and abiding friendships, there is no reason why Pisces and Aquarius can't live together in great harmony though for things to work very well, mutual giving is important.

Pisces needs to rouse itself more and Aquarius must learn to to stay around and listen.

PISCES meets PISCES

This is the last in the list of possible zodiac relationships, which is appropriate because it can easily turn out to be one of the most special. True, Pisces and Pisces don't appear to make great waves – not even ripples on some occasions – but their relationship is one of a latent power and a depth that are utterly incomprehensible to a wealth of other people.

Pisces really does want to understand and to help whenever it can. As a zodiac sign type, it is sometimes deeply misunderstood, however. There is nothing 'soft' about those born under the sign of the Fishes. Some of the bravest and most intrepid individuals the world has ever known were Pisceans. The difference between Pisces and some other zodiac types is that Pisces shows its best face when it is doing what it can to support others. Instinctively, one Piscean will know what makes another tick, so getting to the heart of the matter isn't at all difficult. Friendships of this type will be quiet and mutually supportive and will possess a sort of magnetism that others find extremely potent but difficult to define. Pisceans will also work well together but may not be guaranteed to get a great deal done.

As prospective life partners, Pisceans will appear to be low-key, often distinctly weird and maybe even a little boring. In actual fact, there is a great deal going on beneath the surface of this relationship – to an extent that more materialistic and less sensitive types would find utterly impossible to understand. A degree of excitement regarding interaction with the world at large is likely to be missing, so Pisces and Pisces need mutual friends who can supply it. Trust will be in abundant supply, as will a whole series of common objectives that keep the respective parties busy and happy. However, Pisces and Pisces should definitely avoid withdrawing from a world that can occasionally look threatening. The secret to success for them is to mix freely with the world at large. Children born of this relationship may be somewhat smothered by the affection it can show.

Routines need to be broken and spontaneous action should be welcomed.

Chapter 13
Rising Signs and How to Use Them

ost astrologers agree that, next to the Sun Sign, the most important influence on any person is the Rising Sign at the time of their birth. The Rising Sign represents the astrological sign that was rising over the eastern horizon when each and every one of us came into the world. It is sometimes also called the Ascendant.

Let us suppose, for example, that you were born with the Sun in the zodiac sign of Libra. This would bestow certain characteristics on you that are likely to be shared by all other Librans. However, a Libran with Aries Rising would show a very different attitude towards life, and of course relationships, than a Libran with Pisces Rising.

For these reasons, this book offers a complete section that shows how each zodiac Rising Sign has a bearing on all the possible positions of the Sun at birth. Simply look through the tables that follow this page. Go to the table that is headed with the Sun Sign in which you are interested. (If you are not sure what is meant by your Sun Sign, it is simply that zodiac sign that you refer to for your horoscope in newspapers and magazines and relates to the position of the Sun in the zodiac on the day you were born.) As long as you know the approximate time of birth of the person in whom you are interested, the graph will show you how to discover that individual's Rising Sign.

Look across the top of the graph of your zodiac sign to find your date of birth, and down the side for your birth time (I have used Greenwich Mean Time). Where they cross is your Rising Sign. Don't forget to subtract an hour (or two) if appropriate for Summer Time.

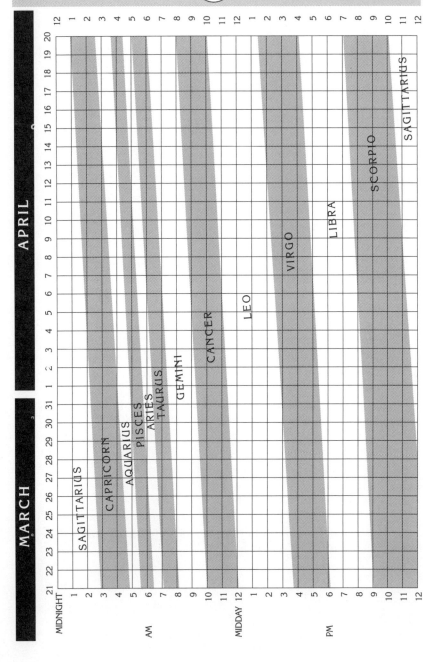

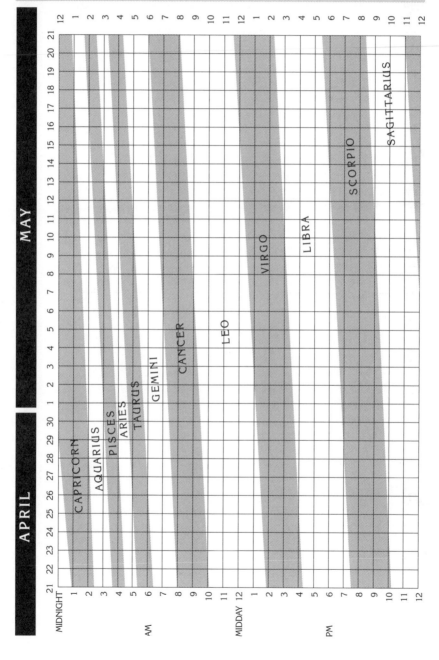

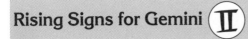
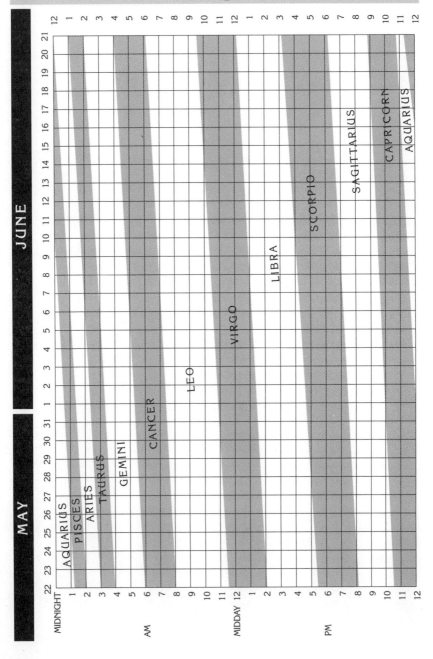

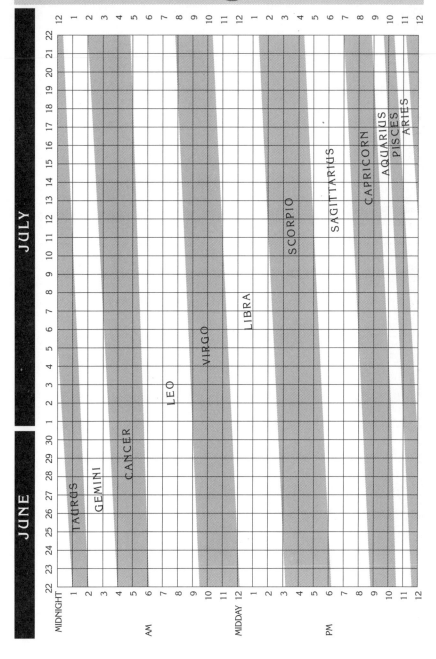

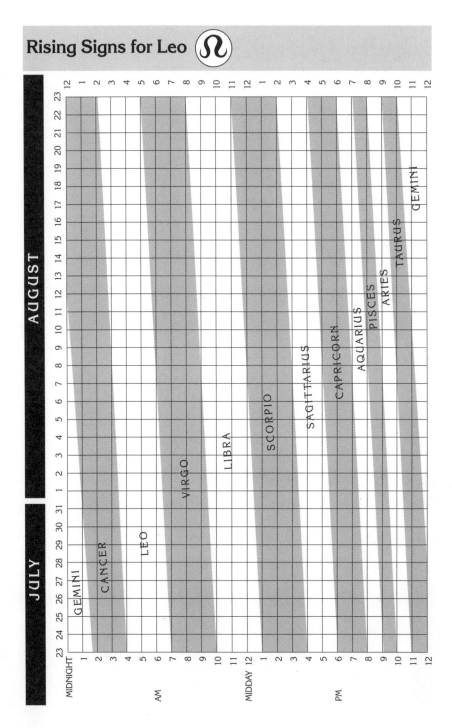

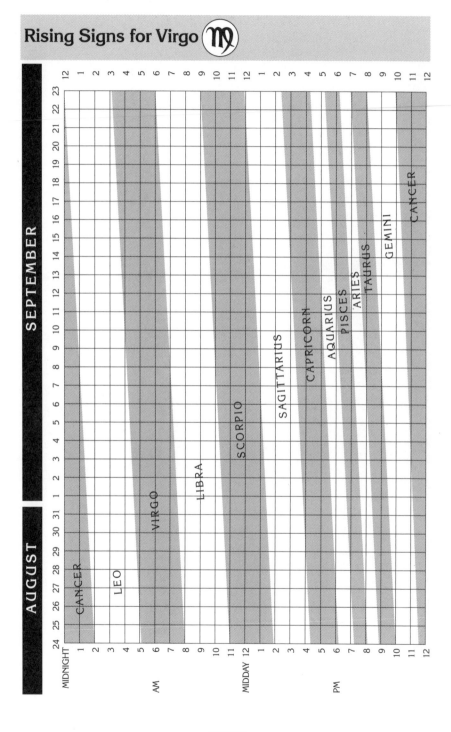

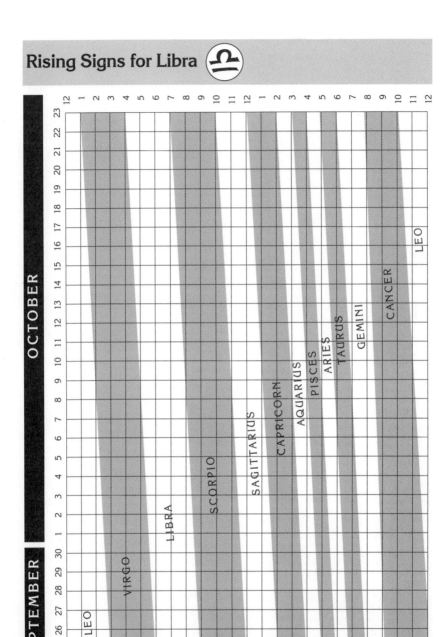

SEPTEMBER OCTOBER

LEO
VIRGO
LIBRA
SCORPIO
SAGITTARIUS
CAPRICORN
AQUARIUS
PISCES
ARIES
TAURUS
GEMINI
CANCER
LEO

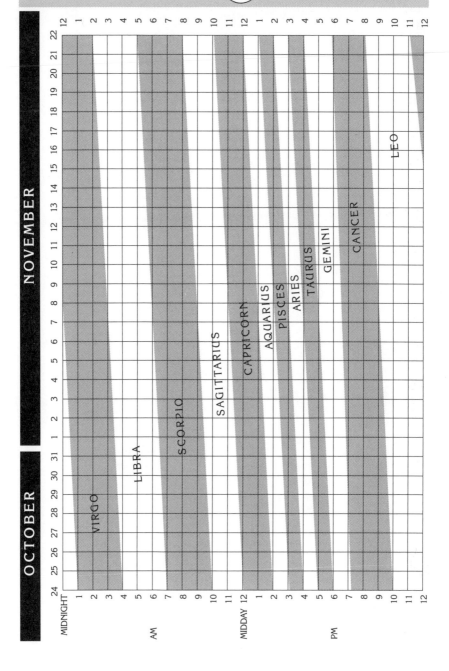

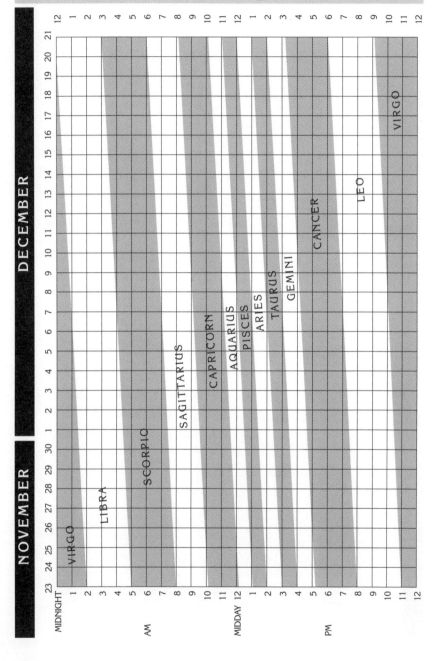

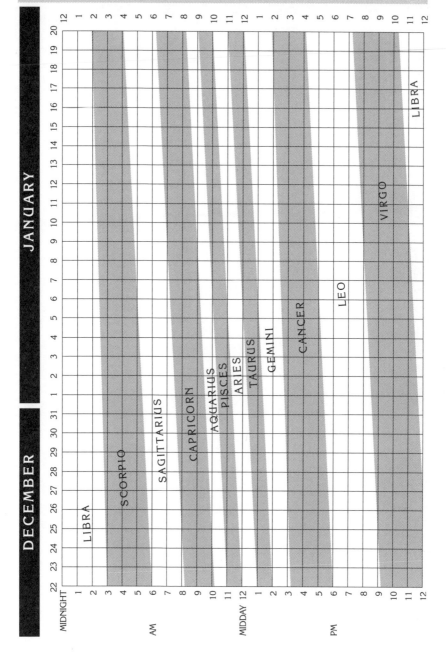

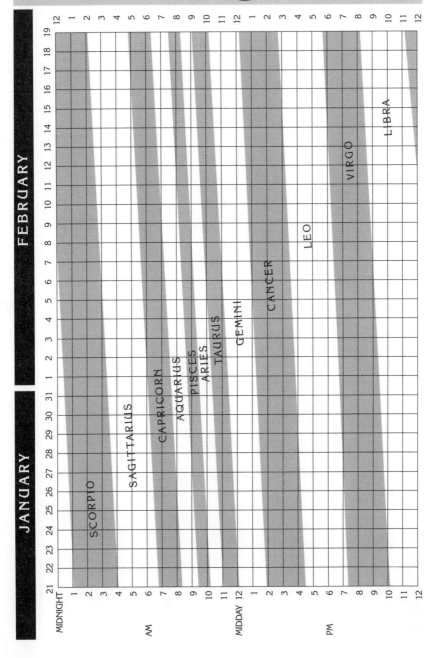

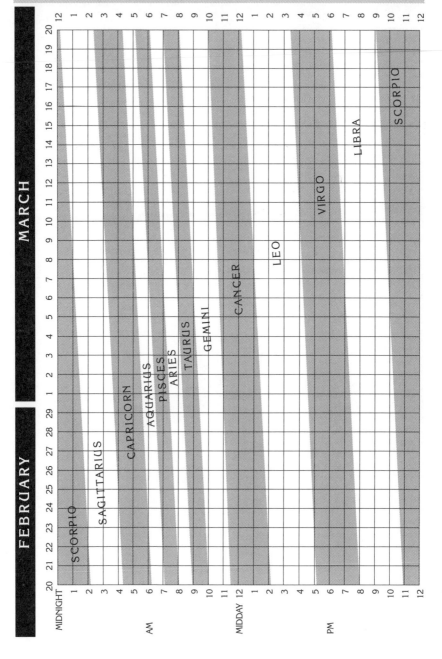

Chapter 14

Rising Signs for Aries

Aries with Aries Rising

This combination indicates a person of great strength and resilience. They are likely to have a no-nonsense approach to life, and may be generally aggressive, particularly in terms of their attitude to work and all practical matters. Aries Rising people are determined and will brook no interference to their plans. It stands to reason, then, that this sort of individual is likely to relate best to people who are either willing to take instructions, or every bit as strong as they are themselves. Even if the latter is true, there are certain to be frequent clashes of will and so a harmonious and easy-going atmosphere may be rather difficult to envisage when dealing with this individual.

Despite the absolute need to be in charge, this is someone who is capable of deep love and almost boundless generosity. When faced with individuals who appear to be vulnerable or in need of assistance, this person can be persuaded to move heaven and earth to please.

Aries with Taurus Rising

Under certain circumstances it would be difficult to envisage this person as a true Aries subject at all, since the nature carries greater refinement and is apt to be quieter than the usual type. There is also more continuity of effort and tremendous staying-power. However, Taurus is what is known as a 'fixed' zodiac sign and so can be very stubborn. Add this to the determination of Aries and here we find a person who, having made up their mind regarding a particular course of action, simply will not be diverted from it.

The secret of success when dealing with this person is to avoid forcing any issue. To do so would, in the end, be a complete waste of time and effort. As in all associations with the sign of the Ram, the way forward is to use understanding and to operate rationally. This individual has a good ability to co-operate with almost any other zodiac sign. Psychology is the key to controlling Aries people who have their Ascendant in Taurus.

Aries with Gemini Rising

Some would suggest that this is one of the busiest of the zodiac combinations but it also proves to be one that creates an essentially entertaining person, though one who retains the essential power of Aries. Here we find someone who communicates well and who wishes to get on with everyone. As a co-worker, the Gemini Rising Aries is adaptable, kind and much more flexible than the Ram taken on its own. Anyone with strong Air-sign tendencies, such as other Geminis, Librans and Aquarians, should find this individual easy to get along with.

When it comes to deeper attachments, we have here a character who finds it somewhat difficult to be faithful in thought, word or deed. This is not to suggest that there is any deliberate duplicity, merely that extra care is necessary when dealing with this person. Expect more humour than the Ram usually demonstrates.

Aries with Cancer Rising

This can turn out to be a very fortunate combination, even if it produces individuals who can sometimes appear to be rather confused as to what their role in life may be. Certainly there is greater warmth than one would expect from Aries when taken alone, together with stronger nurturing tendencies and a definite desire to promote family values and to create a happy home life. Aries with Cancer Rising gives a broader scope for involvement in communal projects, or even simple partnerships. It is warm and affectionate, though with a determined, hard edge that can sometimes appear completely out of the blue. This is a surprising person but not one to be crossed.

Appealing to the better nature of Aries with Cancer Rising is not too difficult and it is sometimes necessary to use a little subterfuge in order to get one's own way. Never directly confront this person – it simply won't work. Better by far to ask for advice and make suggestions.

Aries with Leo Rising

This is a double Fire-sign combination and frequently throws up just about the most dynamic sort of Aries individual of them all. However, unlike Aries with Aries Rising, this individual is quite amenable to reason. Here we find a nobility of spirit and a willingness to use the latent power inherent in the combination for the good of others. This person does not suffer fools gladly, however, and this will include anyone who disagrees with their opinion.

Associating with this type of person is probably not for the faint of heart. In a personal sense, this type of individual is more likely to be paired up with someone who is much less dynamic and who has the sensitivity to deal with the Ram–Lion combination.

Aries with Virgo Rising

Understanding what makes this person tick is the most difficult problem. Aries and Virgo can complement each other in some ways. Together they allow for applied action and create a great deal less aggression than some combinations of zodiac signs allied to Aries. However, Aries is ruled by Mars and Virgo by Mercury – a heady concoction, the sheer force of which could take the wind out of the sails of all but the most prepared. Certainly this person is apt to be talkative, creative, inspirational and very successful when applying its talents sensibly.

The real difficulty may come at a personal level. There are contradictions present in terms of perceived needs, particularly in romance. This breeds a fickle tendency that can be difficult for others to deal with. On the plus side, this is an entertaining nature and one that will always keep others guessing. As with all Aries types, there is great determination and a refusal to compromise when faced with opposition. It is far better to talk rationally to this person than to try and bully them.

Aries with Libra Rising

The addition of Libra has the ability to bring out the very best in almost any zodiac sign and it certainly does so when it is allied to Aries. Here we find an Aries person who is far more willing to give and who demonstrates fairness of nature. None of the Aries ability to get things done is missing but there is a pleasant disposition and also a greater willingness than Aries usually shows to see the other person's point of view and to take it on board.

All the same, these people will be nobody's fool and will not be crossed in matters that they consider to be of the utmost importance. They take time to look at situations and personalities in some depth and decisions are often quite rational and balanced. These are individuals of refinement and good taste.

Aries with Scorpio Rising

Anyone actively wishing to get themselves involved in an emotional maelstrom need look no further than Aries with Scorpio Rising. Both these zodiac signs respond to the planet Mars, though they do so in radically different ways. The most noticeable trait of such individuals is that, though somewhat quieter than the typical Aries subject, they have a tremendous capacity to bear a grudge. This is not an individual who would brook interference and is someone who would clearly make a formidable enemy.

Despite what has been stated above, it should be noted that this combination provides great compassion and a willingness to serve others that amounts to a form of martyrdom. Whether the recipients want to be helped is probably immaterial. To be loved by Aries with Scorpio Rising can be wonderful, though on occasions it may feel stifling. Routines appear to be important on some levels here, though there is an inherent rashness that can be quite difficult to deal with.

Aries with Sagittarius Rising

Although carrying all the power that one would expect of two Fire signs encapsulated within the same nature, Aries with Sagittarius Rising promotes a basically cheerful nature. There is great rush and push about this personality but also an inherent friendliness that isn't always to be found in Aries when taken alone. What matters to this person is that everything is done at breakneck speed. Successes will be frequent, but so will failures. Support is essential for this individual, who functions best when there is constant encouragement.

Life with this type may not be easy and it will certainly be frenetic. However, for those who are capable of sustaining the pace, this is a very interesting proposition. From an economic point of view, Aries with Sagittarius Rising provides both millionaires and paupers.

Aries with Capricorn Rising

It is possible that Capricorn represents the very best levelling influence to Aries. As a result, we find here a very practical person, though one who is also willing to take chances. Somewhat more thoughtful than the average Ram, these individuals are likely to have a greater degree of success with whatever ventures they choose to undertake. Though not exactly friendly, they have a dry and cutting sense of humour and an ability to see through duplicitous types easily.

Aries with Capricorn Rising is not exactly argumentative but can prove to be touchy on occasions and requires careful handling. More than anything, this combination provides a will of iron when it comes to achieving specific objectives. This person is a bulldozer – not as quick as Aries when taken alone, but irrepressible and impossible to control without a good understanding of their emotional base. In romance, expect a deeply physical and practical approach to relationships. Expressing emotion is not at all easy for this person, despite the fact that their feelings run deep.

Aries with Aquarius Rising

This combination can be both magnetic and inspiring, though there are distinct negative aspects that should be understood from the word go. Aries with Aquarius Rising certainly believes it is always right and is not afraid to tell the world. Unfortunately, this is not a combination that learns well through experience as do Aries and Aquarius when taken alone. Still, there is a happy disposition and a love of people. Here we have a deeper nature than the Ram often possesses and Aquarius has a tremendous curiosity. Only the 'fixed' quality of Aquarius holds those born under its sign to a particular topic or subject for long.

Aries with Aquarius Rising tends to be fairly rational, but it may occasionally become entrenched in a particular way of thinking. It is definitely open to suggestion, though it is certainly not credulous. Reasoned discussion works here, whereas direct contradiction will only elicit arguments that are hard to counter.

Aries with Pisces Rising

Here we find a natural understanding of people and situations, allied to an ability to do something constructive. As a result, this combination tends to give rise to individuals who are of great practical use to the world. The personality often seems deeply magnetic and even possesses a mesmeric quality. This is a reasoned thinker who is definitely open to suggestion and who also demonstrates the flexibility one would tend to expect from the Piscean association. A word of warning, however. Once set upon a particular course of action, Aries with Pisces Rising can be just as stubborn as any manifestation of the Ram. This is not a person to be deliberately crossed.

Aries with Pisces Rising spends a great deal of time working on behalf of humanity as a whole. There is compassion, common sense, strength and almost constant activity. Anyone embarking on a romantic attachment with this type has to understand that they will have to share their partner. Selfless determination isn't easy to live with.

Chapter 15
Rising Signs for Taurus

Taurus with Aries Rising

This is an individual who portrays the qualities of Taurus so faithfully that only the really seasoned zodiac watcher would notice the Aries component at first. However, when the chips are down, they can think and act much more quickly than the Bull alone is inclined to do. Added to the natural stubborn quality of Taurus is a great sense of purpose and a determination to win at all costs.

In terms of relationships, it is likely that only in professional associations will one really see the Aries qualities inherent in this nature shining out to any great extent. Nevertheless, these individuals show great courage and can even be foolhardy on occasions. Taurus with Aries Rising is a basically pleasant nature and one that reserves its power, often using it on behalf of less capable types. Not a difficult person to contact socially and someone who knows much about love.

Taurus with Taurus Rising

As might be anticipated, just about everything we would expect of the typical Taurus individual is encapsulated in this nature. Steady, refined, stubborn and yet extremely likeable, this is an individual who is courteous, often quiet but very powerful when roused to action. At almost any level, the world will find this person to be accommodating and easily influenced by kindness. There are strong artistic qualities here and a need to make the world into a tidier and more ordered place.

Taurus with Taurus Rising inclines to harmony, making this an interesting and placid person most of the time. Only when under severe stress or when faced with the problems suffered by others will this individual show the true mettle of their nature. In love, this is an ardent and very sincere type, someone who cares deeply and who proves this fact over and over again in small ways. It would be hard to imagine Taurus with Taurus Rising causing a scene, either socially or personally.

Taurus with Gemini Rising

This is undoubtedly one of the most pleasant combinations for an individual born with the Sun in Taurus. The presence of Gemini here tends to broaden the outlook and makes for a more flamboyant and happy-go-lucky individual than would be the case with Taurus viewed alone. Taurus with Gemini Rising tends to lead to great success and a willingness to take chances. This person is easy to get to know – and to like. Powers of communication are likely to be good and the overall success rating is usually very high.

Above all, Taurus with Gemini Rising is optimistic and is less inclined to brood than the Bull on occasions. Some of the brashness of Gemini is present and so is a great deal of the charm and wit of this most capricious of the Air signs.

Taurus with Cancer Rising

This is a very quiet Taurean indeed and one who knows the value of keeping to a steady and well-defined path in life. It would be extraordinary to find this person in a grumpy or unpleasant state of mind unless circumstances were really bad. As a friend, they will be loyal to the bitter end, though their support will tend to be shown in quiet ways. A worker behind the scenes, Taurus with Cancer Rising has an innate sense of what looks and feels right, together with strong artistic inclinations and a fondness for nature in all its forms.

There are better travel prospects here than may be expected with Taurus taken alone, together with a need to plumb the depths of emotional experience. This person is not especially adventurous but is certainly open to suggestion and will take a chance, particularly if the well-being of others is at stake. Good with money, Taurus with Cancer Rising tends to achieve what it wants, though perhaps after some pitfalls. The best way to describe this personality might simply be 'extremely likeable'.

Taurus with Leo Rising

The presence of Leo in the Taurean nature adds bite and determination. This is a sunny, warm and generally optimistic type who is far less likely to brood over situations than the standard Taurean. 'Considered action' is the key to this individual's nature and it is true that when they decide on a particular course of action they will brook no interference. The stubborn qualities of Taurus are definitely to be found here, even if they manifest themselves in a much more positive way, for example in defence of others, rather than merely defending itself.

Taurus with Leo Rising brings a level of sociability that is easy for all to see. As a rule, we find in this person someone who doesn't have any difficulty making or keeping friends. There is something particularly brave about them, together with a noble quality that might be seen as slightly out of date, but nevertheless attractive.

Taurus with Virgo Rising

There isn't much doubt that this is one of the quietest of the Taurean Rising Signs. Virgo tends to be garrulous and friendly but in this case is somewhat stifled beneath the quieter Taurean influence. One of the advantages of the mix is its ingenuity, which displays itself in steady but definite ways. This is a person who can keep going for a long time, even when the journey is protracted and the effort seems to be extreme. In terms of relationships with others, Taurus with Virgo Rising is loyal, though with a slight tendency to bitch about certain friends and family members.

To know this person deeply is not easy. As a result, the combination is likely to appeal to far more gregarious types, usually people who have an insatiable curiosity. There is something deeply physical about Taurus with Virgo Rising, especially in terms of personal relationships. This combination breeds staying-power, together with great intensity and a need for love that sometimes remains unfulfilled. Although getting really close to this character is difficult, the results will be worth the effort.

Taurus with Libra Rising

What makes this combination so very attractive is the fact that both Taurus and Libra are ruled by the planet Venus. As a result, it would be difficult to imagine a more cultured, artistic or generally affable nature. This person is neither quiet nor noisy, but simply responds to prevailing circumstances. It might be suggested that here we find the perfect friend, partner or consort. Taurus with Libra Rising would run a mile sooner than create an embarrassing or difficult situation for anyone and yet can get its message across in a way that is difficult to ignore.

Routines do not bother Taurus with Libra Rising. All tasks tend to be undertaken with the same sense of patience, though not if they are dirty or unsavoury in any way. This last is not important, however, for these individuals have little or no difficulty in persuading others to undertake those chores they don't care for.

Taurus with Scorpio Rising

This is a deceptively powerful nature and not a person to be crossed in any way. Although quiet and deeply reserved under most circumstances, there is a latent energy here that can shock the world if it is released. Vitality may seem to be lacking and there is a definite lazy streak, with a sensuous love of luxury and probably a tendency to overeat on occasions. All in all, the world can easily be lulled into a false sense of security, pigeon-holing this individual without getting to know what lies below the surface.

In fact, this individual can demonstrate a burning passion, great resilience and an ability to fight long after everyone else has given up the struggle and gone home. It is almost impossible to defeat Taurus with Scorpio Rising, but fortunately there is no need to attempt the exercise. This is a person who can easily be persuaded by a sensible and rational argument. The combination brings a brave ally of unquestionable loyalty.

Taurus with Sagittarius Rising

It would be hard to dislike this type. True, some of the deception of Sagittarius is present, though it is never likely to be used in a malicious or totally selfish way, unless there is extreme pressure forcing the issue. The Taurean ability to work hard is complemented by the fact that Sagittarius brings good communication skills and an overall desire for material success. For this reason, Taurus with Sagittarius Rising may seem to offer less in terms of personal relationships. Work is more likely to stimulate this type but concerted effort will find the essential heart of the combination.

This zodiac mixing is less concerned with detail than the fastidious Bull sometimes seems to be, and is more likely to deal in approximations. Only on occasions does the slightly lazy side of Taurus manifest itself. This sign combination also tends to create good travellers who revel in new experiences.

Taurus with Capricorn Rising

The most capable combination for Taurus in terms of all practicalities. Taurus knows how to think about doing, but Capricorn has the knowledge to put those thoughts into practice. Taurus with Capricorn Rising doesn't provide for a particularly gregarious nature, though the individual born under it is almost certain to be pleasant, kind and considerate. There is great style and breeding, though this is coloured with more than a hint of the common touch that comes from the sign of the Goat.

Don't underestimate this type. If they wish to make mountains out of molehills, they will find a way to accomplish the task. When it comes to building a home, they could probably do the job from the ground up. Partnerships are difficult with this combination but once a trust is established it is usually in place for good. Pursuing a personal relationship may be even harder but nobody could ask for a more loyal or loving partner and few would shun the material success they bring.

Taurus with Aquarius Rising

Ingenious, interesting, intellectual and unique – all of these are accurate descriptions of Taurus with Aquarius Rising when it is working at its best. The presence of Aquarius makes for a rather outgoing sort of Taurean and one who exhibits a tremendous curiosity about the world. Here we find good administrative capabilities and a sense of togetherness that makes this a charming character to know. From friendship through to a much deeper, romantic attachment, this is an easy person to like and you may find in them a loyal friend and a source of endless interest.

Understanding them may be rather more difficult because Taurus with Aquarius rising is quirky and sometimes erratic. The two signs create a happy nature but they don't mix entirely well, leaving the observer noticing very definite Taurean trends, such as that famous stubborn streak, and yet on other occasions an absolute need for variety.

Taurus with Pisces Rising

There is no doubt that this is one of the most pleasant manifestations of Taurus, but it is not a combination that is either gregarious or easy to get to know. Pisces brings a much deeper and more reflective quality to the Bull, imposing on it a great sense of social duty but not endowing it with particularly sociable ways. In some ways it is the least favourable combination for either zodiac sign and yet it has many redeeming qualities, some of which would only be fully recognised from within a respected friendship or a more personal attachment.

Taurus with Pisces Rising offers great genuine emotion to the Bull and also endows it with a deeper intuition. Understanding what makes others tick is second nature to these individuals, though since they very rarely share their insights with the world at large, a great percentage of their talents tend to be wasted. There is nothing remotely impulsive here and the very essence of this nature is towards conservatism and caution.

Chapter 16

Rising Signs for Gemini

Gemini with Aries Rising

With this combination we find exactly the same sort of general affability that comes with Gemini when taken alone. However, in addition there is very much more 'bite' to the nature and a determination to succeed that is far stronger than that often exhibited by the sign of the Twins. Geminis with Aries Rising are more inclined to succeed in life and may show themselves as being somewhat ruthless in their activities, particularly in a work situation.

This is not a difficult combination either to understand or to get on with, because Gemini people of almost any type are friendly and approachable. In fact, it might be suggested that people born under Gemini with Aries Rising are less fickle and usually more loyal than most, and have greater concentration generally. The combination is also likely to bring good financial prospects.

Gemini with Taurus Rising

This combination tends to add extra refinement and even more affability to the Gemini nature. Look out for a strongly artistic quality and a greater tendency to be tidy than appears to be the case with Gemini taken alone. This makes this person easier to get on with, particularly when associated with Earth signs, such as Taurus and Virgo. Here we find an extremely pleasant individual, maybe somewhat quieter than Gemini often tends to be, yet imbued with a disarming ability to say and do exactly the right thing, particularly in a romantic situation.

For any sort of working association, this is a naturally positive combination because it inclines people to be even more adaptable than Gemini normally tends to be. Good powers of concentration are added to its storehouse of natural abilities and there is no lack of insight at a deep level. Gemini with Taurus Rising knows how to love and is usually quite sincere. Almost any individual who meets this person will find them easy to get on with, truthful and utterly charming.

Gemini with Gemini Rising

Here we find a person who – not surprisingly – tends to be absolutely typical of Gemini in every way. This brings a host of benefits to the nature, though one or two difficulties as well. Gemini with Gemini Rising is charming, talkative, interested in anyone and everyone, never bears a grudge and is easy to get to know. Life is never dull around this character but the sheer force and dynamism of the person is difficult for some people to deal with, simply because it is like being around a whirlwind. Still, it is hard to dislike this individual, who, at the very worst, is a loveable rogue.

Double Gemini is great for friendship and also for working relationships, at least under most circumstances. Real problems may arise in deeper attachments, simply because Gemini is not the most loyal or constant sort of individual. Plenty of diversion is required, together with a knowledge that there is no cage, either real or mental, to fetter this irrepressible and often stunning personality.

Gemini with Cancer Rising

Quite simply, many people will say that, all things considered, this is one of the most charming and easy-going individuals they have ever met. Here we find a person who seems to have conquered the less acceptable qualities of Gemini and has, instead, inherited a steadier and calmer way to display the sign of the Twins to the world. Communication is no problem to this type, though the chatterbox mentality that comes with some Gemini people may not be noticeable. There is more sympathy and constancy, together with a greater practical use of intuition.

Gemini with Cancer Rising people remain quite faithful and are easy to get along with at just about any level. With no lack of depth and plenty of patience, they provide an ideal friend, business partner or lover for many other zodiac sign combinations. Nobody is perfect, but this type comes remarkably close.

Gemini with Leo Rising

The Gemini who also has Leo in his or her own nature is more likely to be able to finish whatever projects they embark upon. In addition, this is an individual who finds it easy to occupy any sort of executive role. Gemini with Leo Rising promotes people who are loyal, bold and often forthright. Anyone looking for someone who will readily fall in line should, perhaps, avoid this combination of zodiac signs because this type is far less likely to compromise than Gemini when taken alone.

In love, this person is likely to be quite sincere; they have better staying-power at every level than most other combinations of Gemini and enjoy a bright and sunny personality most of the time. The accent is on activity at every level, with the result that some would find this individual just too exuberant.

Gemini with Virgo Rising

Although more practical and capable than Gemini when taken alone, the combination with Virgo can bring its own particular difficulties. The nature is inspirational, with even a touch of genius on occasions.

Both Gemini and Virgo are ruled by chatty Mercury, so there will be no lack of conversation from this individual. In addition, the person may be a fluent and keen writer. With deep insights into the way others think, Gemini with Virgo Rising can be disarming and sometimes a little spooky in the way they frequently manage to jump to the right conclusions. At work, this person can show great application and an 'across the board' series of skills that may create the ideal employee or workmate.

Love them or hate them, Gemini with Virgo Rising individuals will not be ignored. They have very specific views about a range of matters, though are usually willing to see an alternative point of view if talked to considerately. Most of all, they hate unfairness.

Gemini with Libra Rising

Many Gemini types will jump with ease from one task to another. What sets Gemini with Libra Rising apart is the fact that they try to balance everything and do it all at once. Most of the time this works quite well but this is an individual who, at heart, is probably quite nervy and lives life on the edge. The harmonious and easy-going qualities of Libra sit well with the affable and talkative Gemini personality, though there can be an inherent superficiality that some people find awkward to accommodate. This character is unlikely to take life too seriously, despite the fact that they have an innate sense of justice and right.

Almost anyone can live comfortably around Gemini with Libra Rising, if only because there are few areas for argument. Less contentious than many Gemini types, this person would do almost anything to avoid falling out with the world at large.

Gemini with Scorpio Rising

Some people will find this individual a strange fish at almost any level. This is Gemini – but with a depth and an attitude that is sometimes odd and may even be downright peculiar. At times, the person will seem to be extremely friendly, with an ability to disarm the most awkward types. There is even a degree of superficiality – though this is probably an illusion. But beneath the surface lies a penetrating insight into what people can be and a latent power that some would think to be rather spooky.

At heart, Gemini with Scorpio Rising wants to care for everyone, which is fine as long as the person in question really wants to be looked after. At worst, this type is nosy and interfering, with a tendency to monopolise friends and lovers. Still, there is a warmth and sincerity here that far surpasses Gemini when taken alone, together with a great affability in almost any situation. A person who is definitely better for knowing and one who will be cherished more with every passing day.

Gemini with Sagittarius Rising

There is nothing remotely deep about these characters, which is one of the reasons why they are so easy to get on with. Talkative, capable, boastful and yet utterly charming, this is the sort of person with whom most individuals would want to spend their social hours. In any group situation, Gemini with Sagittarius Rising holds the floor and is the most natural public speaker in the world. As a buddy, a relative or a workmate, this character tends to be the best, even if a great deal of energy is required simply to keep up with their lightning thought processes and actions.

When it comes to deeper attachments, some care is necessary. Neither Gemini nor Sagittarius promotes faithfulness. As long as this character has plenty to think about and does not become bored, they will be the most charming partner imaginable, though will sometimes move on when the romance requires too much effort.

Gemini with Capricorn Rising

Practical application, when allied to Gemini adaptability, is certainly a sign of success. What is more, this type has the personality to add spark to almost any situation. In the workplace, Gemini with Capricorn Rising provides someone who is easy to get along with but whose ability to do almost anything can be distressing to some. This is a real character and someone who can turn their hand – or head – to almost any sort of situation and come up with a practical answer.

It is hard to envisage anyone really finding fault with this type. Capricorn brings a degree of depth, toning down some of the more forthright and talkative qualities of Gemini, though without removing the affability or charm. In personal relationships, Gemini with Capricorn Rising is sincere and less likely to be unfaithful than other types of Gemini. This person would never forget a birthday or duck out when it comes to doing practical things around the home. Probably the ideal partner, in the view of many.

Gemini with Aquarius Rising

This is someone who is able to get on with the world at large in almost any way, and who enjoys a high degree of popularity. Aquarius doesn't exhibit quite the degree of superficiality that is often the case with Gemini taken alone, and is much more inclined to look more deeply into specific situations. Gemini does not lose its natural charm, or its ability to communicate at almost any level when it mixes with fellow Air sign Aquarius. It remains chatty but loses its tendency to be vulgar or backbiting and can be flexible and friendly without degenerating into flightiness. The natural qualities of the sign are refined and tempered, probably producing a more rounded and positive character.

Under certain circumstances, this person can be quite forthright, though generally only when sticking up for others. Constancy in personal attachments may not be particularly great, if only because the curiosity bestowed by this combination brings a need to move on and to challenge old values.

Gemini with Pisces Rising

Gemini sometimes lacks a cohesive direction and tends to spread itself too thinly across life, and the situation as apt to be made worse when the sign of Pisces is part of the scenario. Nevertheless, this is one of the most pleasant individuals almost anyone is likely to meet. Pisces has a degree of inner beauty, which when allied to Gemini's natural traits can be immensely attractive. Often quite handsome physically, Gemini with Pisces Rising has a disarming quality and an ability to understand what makes other people tick. However, it fails to come to terms with its view of its own personality, because there is a distinct lack of self-appreciation.

Almost any relationship with this individual is stimulating. Sensitive types will recognise an intuitive quality that is second to none, allied to an innate ability to help out when people are in trouble. There is something 'other-worldly' about this type of person, a quality that many will love but which others will find too nebulous for comfort.

Chapter 17
Rising Signs for Cancer

Cancer with Aries Rising

Although a decisive and positive combination in some respects, this type brings certain difficulties to anyone involved with this individual. The zodiac sign of Cancer has a strong desire to nurture, a proclivity that is still in place when Aries is the Rising Sign. The problem arises when this desire becomes stifling and overprotective. Not everyone finds this an easy quality to deal with. In other respects, we find a determined and decisive sort of Cancerian, someone who is sensitive, reliable and positive. The general quality of nature is not diminished and the likeable Cancer nature remains intact.

The natural home-building tendencies of the Crab are assisted here by better practical skills and a slightly more outgoing nature, allowing greater social diversion and better executive skill. This person is easy to get to know and like.

Cancer with Taurus Rising

The presence of the zodiac sign of Taurus in this nature does little or nothing to overpower the general Cancerian traits. This individual will work long and hard to support family and friends and is ardent, sincere and loving. The presence of Taurus strengthens the resolve and adds extra artistic qualities to the nature, at the same time making this person more stubborn than would typically be the case for the sign of Cancer. In terms of friendship, we find a loyal, understanding and co-operative individual – not especially outgoing but approachable.

Taurus Rising may bring a slightly more dry sense of humour and greater abilities to address practical matters. This is not someone who will relish dirty tasks, though for the sake of those it loves, Cancer with Taurus Rising will undertake almost anything. It would be hard to dislike this individual but they are never going to be the noisiest person in any room and they are difficult to get to know. Patience is necessary in the early stages of any attachment here.

Cancer with Gemini Rising

In this combination, we frequently find Cancerian subjects who are more at ease with themselves than is sometimes the case with Cancer when taken alone. The reason is simple. The inclusion of Gemini Rising in the nature makes for better powers of communication and a greater ability to diversify. These are individuals who tend to be quite at ease with the world at large and yet retain the depth, sensitivity and understanding that is an inherent part of those born under the sign of the Crab.

This person often has a nature that stands midway between the chatty, carefree qualities that typify the sign of the Twins, and the introspective worrying of Cancer. The result is a nature that is invariably balanced, extremely friendly and yet capable of great insights.

Cancer with Cancer Rising

Everything that is good and some things that are less than fortunate about the zodiac sign of Cancer are brought together and made more noticeable in the case of the double Cancerian individual. The subject remains friendly, protective and extremely fond of home and family and in every way gives evidence of much caring for the world at large. The presence of Cancer Rising does tend to increase the protective instincts, mainly due to a greater tendency to worry than is the case with Cancer in isolation.

Perhaps this individual shows a fondness for routines, or is less inclined to travel. Certainly, we find here a desire for what is known and understood. It is very difficult to dislike any double Cancer type, even though they are not always easy to comprehend. Quiet and sometimes broody, double Cancer is usually only thinking up better ways to love and protect those people it cares for. This combination usually allies itself with far more dynamic types.

Cancer with Leo Rising

The presence of Leo in this nature opens up the personality like a bright and fragrant flower, allowing most of what is good about the sign of Cancer to express itself in a more positive way to the world at large. Leo adds determination to the nature and also increases the social qualities of an already friendly and approachable zodiac sign. These individuals rarely seek trouble and yet there is a latent ability to see matters through to their logical conclusion, even in the face of adversity or argument.

Cancer with Leo rising is eminently reasonable and will always take the line of least resistance if it is possible to do so. Nevertheless, this is basically a strong character. It will not be bullied or coerced and knows how to achieve its objectives. Cancer with Leo rising makes a steadfast, loyal and protective partner or friend.

Cancer with Virgo Rising

In terms of practical know-how, this person is second to none. Socially, they appear to be far more extroverted than actually turns out to be the case. Communication skills seem good, but there is a quiet and sometimes brooding interior to them that is difficult for many to understand. The presence of Virgo does much to make Cancer more practical but can sometimes lessen the depth of understanding that is an inherent quality within those ruled by the sign of the Crab. To compensate, the nature is very insightful and perhaps also more structured.

To gain the trust of this type of Cancerian may not be easy, though once this is accomplished such an individual will make a staunch, if somewhat nosy, friend. At a deeper level, it might be suggested that this is the type of person who will choose a romantic attachment very carefully and rescind it only after long consideration. Beware a nature that may be too fond of routine and which can become staid. This individual may need encouragement to take life less seriously.

Cancer with Libra Rising

If it is fairness and equilibrium you seek, look no further than Cancer with Libra Rising. This is a nature very much at ease with itself, and the combination makes for a more successful life overall than either Cancer or Libra would bring alone. Look out for an old-fashioned sense of right and wrong and a great desire for things to be just and honourable. Overlay these tendencies with a bright, happy, sociable but not overly noisy character and it becomes obvious that this is a combination that works.

Nobody is perfect of course. Cancer with Libra Rising finds it hard to make decisions, because taking on board the considerations of everyone is impossible. Nevertheless, there is a lightness of touch present and, perhaps surprisingly, executive ability.

Cancer with Scorpio Rising

Below the surface of this generally friendly, happy and easy-going type lies an interior that is almost impossible to fathom for all but the most persistent and perceptive individuals. It is possible to know the Cancer with Scorpio Rising type for many years and still not get to the core of a potential that often remains unfulfilled in a number of ways. It may be that these individuals are placing limitations on their means of expression, or, alternatively, it may be that to allow the absolute sensitivity of both the Crab and Scorpion to surface would prove too threatening to the individual. Either way, this is an intriguing person, but in terms of a deep attachment is not to be taken lightly.

Invariably charming, with a good ability to work hard, Cancer with Scorpio Rising is deeply committed to home and family and will eventually feel thwarted if it cannot feel settled and content. Although not naturally gregarious, this type is brave at a physical level and will often participate in quite dangerous sporting activities. Natural attractiveness is usually present, together with a sort of mystique. Easy to love but very hard to understand fully – that's Cancer with Scorpio Rising.

Cancer with Sagittarius Rising

This turns out to be a most unusual combination and one that can manifest itself in a number of ways. Sagittarius is generally taken to be a superficial sign, and Cancer is one of the deepest. However, the qualities of these two signs mix about as well as oil and water, the result being a nature that varies, according to the different spheres of life. This person is likely to be charming by nature, apparently friendly, talkative and interested in others and yet, in family terms, may be known as quiet and retiring. In other words, Cancer with Sagittarius Rising puts life into compartments.

This tendency shows itself on many different levels, making for a complex nature that is difficult to understand fully. None of this detracts from the fact that this type can be utterly fascinating, deeply attractive and generally magnetic.

Cancer with Capricorn Rising

These signs are opposites on the zodiac wheel and yet in some respects present themselves to the world in a fairly similar way. Thus the person who combines them possesses not only the good qualities but also the less positive traits inherent to both signs. Sensitive, as all Cancerians tend to be, this individual not only worries about loved ones but is able to do much to assist at a practical level. Easy-going and kind, Cancer with Capricorn Rising often displays a great, though dry, sense of humour. The presence of the sign of the Goat stiffens the Cancerian resolve and makes the change and travel Cancer needs a more practical proposition.

Capricorn is robust and known to be a creative, practical zodiac sign that likes to do things with its hands. Its presence here allows Cancer to be more intrepid and may also strengthen its nerve. To many, this individual will make an excellent friend or partner. In terms of political, economic or religious beliefs this type generally attempts to remain neutral. This sort of Cancerian is not over-complicated or demanding.

Cancer with Aquarius Rising

Aquarius tends to bring a refreshing twist to the basic Cancerian nature, imbuing it with originality, verve and an ability to communicate well with the world at large. This individual shows a great interest in life at many different levels and will definitely brighten the world for friends, of whom it has a great many. With a fascination for the odd, the unusual and the downright weird, Cancer with Aquarius Rising is charismatic, unprepossessing and yet rarely radical.

As a friend, this sign combination can be second to none. Here we find care and concern, though they are rarely expressed in a cloying manner. Constancy of the usual Cancerian type may be in doubt, but entertainment and interest certainly aren't.

Cancer with Pisces Rising

Cancer with Pisces Rising often allies itself to Fire-sign types, such as Aries or Leo. Here it finds the support and protection it needs and a good conduit for its own strengths.

This nature might be altogether too deep for some types to understand. The presence of Pisces forces the Cancerian nature even further down within itself, making communication with the world at large difficult. To counteract this tendency, Cancer with Pisces Rising may promote one of the most understanding natures to be found anywhere. These people love ardently and are natural homemakers for the world at large. They often give themselves totally in service to humanity, and their sheer selflessness is extremely laudable – though not everyone's cup of tea.

Dedication is the hallmark of this combination. The nature is pleasant, cultured and extremely kind, with a natural dislike of discord. At a personal level, a relationship with this combination can sometimes be like living with a sensitive plant, which shrinks away at the merest touch. There are rewards, however, since this is the most selfless giver of all the Rising Sign combinations for Cancer.

Chapter 18

Rising Signs for Leo

Leo with Aries Rising

This is a character who is full of get up and go, rarely stuck for a positive word or action and absolutely committed to getting on in life. Leo with Aries Rising wants to be at the front of the queue in life but does have nobility and a sense of honour, the most important hallmarks of the Leo type.

This individual makes a sterling and loyal friend, though they may set high standards that would not be easy for some people to live up to. Here we find the Leo ability to get on well with others, yet there is a sort of arrogance that is difficult to deal with and a sense of purpose that may make this person difficult to equal or better.

Not at all the sort of person who would be easily discouraged, it would take a very adventurous individual to keep up with, let alone better, Leo with Aries Rising.

Leo with Taurus Rising

Leo is bright, adventurous, bold and regal. All these are traits that ally themselves quite well to the much less dynamic Bull. As a result, we find a Leo who is more willing to listen and who shows a far more artistic temperament. Leos with Taurus Rising are not at all likely to back the wrong horse in any race; they have good executive ability, backed up by a willingness to listen, but they also possess a will of iron. This is a combination that could be held by the first soldier over the top and the last sports star to quit.

Not everyone finds Leo with Taurus Rising all that easy to get along with, if only because there is an innate sense of stubbornness here that can be difficult to counter. All the same there is much to set this individual apart and potential financial success is one strong point. Relationships are often formed with less positive types and these people have a strong protective quality and a desire to please. They find it easier to deal with routines than would be the case with Leo taken alone and we also discover some practical skills that actually allow these Leos to get things done around the house.

Leo with Gemini Rising

This is Leo with the common touch. Not half so grand as Leo when taken alone, this character is more willing to muck in and can be found at the front in any social situation. Routines are tedious to them and the desire for change and diversity is very strong indeed. Not a person to be countered in argument, Leo with Gemini Rising is always right.

Although Gemini people are inclined to talk about anything – whether they understand the subject or not – this is much less so when the zodiac sign is allied to Leo. On the contrary, there is real power in what this person says, allied to the necessary skill to put words into action. A fearless orator.

Leo with Cancer Rising

Here we find Leo with a strong conscience and even an overwhelming desire to help humanity. The Lion is always noble but the presence of the sign of Cancer adds to the depth of someone who could otherwise be accused of being superficial. Leo with Cancer Rising genuinely does want to help and is particularly protective of relatives and friends. The sunny, warm disposition of Leo is assisted by the fact that Cancer works well on an emotional level, something that the Lion often cannot do.

Also more adaptable than Leo when taken alone, Leo with Cancer Rising is willing to take orders, but is just as capable of handing them out. Don't be surprised to find this character starting working life in a lowly position but ending up chairing the board. As a life partner, this individual knows how to be faithful but still manages to find the right words of love, even decades after the relationship has begun. It is said that Leos with Cancer Rising have a strong physique and they can usually be relied upon to be hard at work, even when everyone else has gone home. Not as noisy as the Lion sometimes tends to be, there is a tendency for deep thought here, which is refreshing.

Leo with Leo Rising

It would be hard to fail to realise what is on offer with this combination, no matter what sort of relationship is up for grabs. Leo is sunny, warm, candid, brave, adventurous and yet, paradoxically, capable of being very lazy. All these are qualities that can be expected to turn up on cue when Leo meets Leo Rising. These are individuals who expect much of themselves, and though kind, may also imagine that the rest of the world can turn in the same sort of performance.

Utterly charming and also quite disarming, Leo with Leo Rising will rarely fail to please. Although sometimes accused of being rather shallow, Leos have a good line in romance and love to take responsibility for their partner. Loyalty comes naturally and there is great potential for excitement.

Leo with Virgo Rising

Perhaps not the most fortunate combination for Leo, since Virgo is such a very different sort of zodiac sign. There are benefits, however. Leo is not usually all that well organised and functions half the time by acting on instinct. With Virgo in place as well, we find a Leo type who can plan in addition to getting things done. Extremely sociable and very willing to please, this person can also be given to unusually quiet spells, which will often come as a shock to anyone who doesn't know this individual well.

The natural volatility of Leo is slowed here and sometimes manifests itself as a sort of brooding, which is not typical of the Lion as a rule. Nevertheless, the powers of communication are stimulated and this is a person who can be a real evangelist regarding almost anything that is held as being special or sacred.

There is latent power on offer from Leo with Virgo Rising, even if on occasions it takes some time to show itself. Maybe not the easiest person to live with – but great fun. Friends with this combination can entertain almost anyone they take to.

Leo with Libra Rising

If there is one thing that Leo lacks, it is the ability to see the other person's point of view. Libra assists this slightly less-than-perfect quality in the Lion and provides an individual who is more than willing to take a second look at practically any issue. The warm and happy Leo nature will be present as ever, but made more artistic and flexible by the sign of the Scales. Beware a tendency to chatter a great deal, however.

Almost anyone can get on with this type, because there is sufficient interest present to create a person who is stimulated by diversity. However, Leos with Libra Rising can become bored and then tend to wander off in search of other stimulation. Routines can seem a chore and this sort of character thrives on travel.

Leo with Scorpio Rising

This is one powerful person – difficult to understand and impossible to place in any sort of category. Scorpio is an extremely deep zodiac sign and may not mix too well with the sunny superficiality of Leo. However, there are similarities that are strengthened by the match. Both signs tend to be very brave, even foolhardy on occasions. Physically speaking, there is strength and power, but perhaps also a slight tendency towards hypochondria that others find strange.

Leo with Scorpio Rising wants to be popular, even if achieving this objective can sometimes prove more difficult for this sort of Lion. Loyalty, always the hallmark of the Lion, is strengthened considerably with this contact, and personal relationships are taken extremely seriously. Actually understanding what makes this individual tick is the hardest part and may prove to be an exercise that will span a lifetime. There's no real answer because Leo with Scorpio Rising doesn't know either.

Great gains are on offer for anyone getting together with this type – though a few problems too. Not the simplest combination of zodiac signs but well worth a second look.

Leo with Sagittarius Rising

Two Fire signs such as these, when allied, can make for an interesting combination, and there are few quite so magnetic as Leo with Sagittarius Rising. In almost every sphere where either Leo or Sagittarius is deficient, the strengths in the other sign come to the rescue. For example, Sagittarius can be flighty and inclined to skip from one situation to another. Leo brings greater constancy, but doesn't overpower the naturally winning ways that are part of the Archer's nature.

At the level of friendship, this is someone that most people would want to know. Often good-looking, always self-assured, it would be hard to find a more likeable soul, though also difficult to discover one who could get away with being so immodest, whilst at the same time remaining so affable. Definitely a handful.

Leo with Capricorn Rising

The presence of Capricorn Rising in a Leo chart is certain to influence some of the most gregarious impulses of the Lion. At the same time, it brings a greater sense of conservatism, allied to genuine practicality that makes for a Lion that is creative, inspirational and unusual. There is terrific originality locked into this combination, together with a desire for an unusual lifestyle and capabilities that span a broad range of potentials. Don't expect too much in the way of peace and quiet when Leo with Capricorn Rising gets busy around the house.

If you are looking for the sort of partner who decides in the morning that there are one too many walls in the house, and who then has the offending structure knocked down before lunchtime, you will get on well with this combination. Their wit is dry and deliberate and their level of intelligence usually very high. Although able to get on with the world at large, Leo with Capricorn Rising prefers the unusual and may travel to, and choose to live in, some exotic and possibly remote location.

Leo with Aquarius Rising

Although this combination doesn't possess quite the same level of practical skills as Leo with Capricorn Rising, it is every bit as original and probably downright odd. Aquarius is the sign of the revolutionary – the sort of person who wants to know everything about the way the world works and then to change it. Aquarius rarely gets round to doing so, though when it is the Rising Sign of Leo, there is great scope for action and little reservation about who knows it.

This character has time for idle chat, but little is lost on what turns out to be a razor-sharp mind. With strength of character, yet an extremely flexible approach to most situations, Leo with Aquarius Rising is up for action and only too willing to have a good time. There are great gains to be had from knowing this person.

Leo with Pisces Rising

Although the presence of Pisces slows considerably some of the more impetuous ways of the progressive Lion, it brings to the sign a form of quiet nobility that almost everyone will find particularly attractive. At times deep and awkward to fathom, Leo with Pisces Rising can seem moody and even quiet. Actually, there are periods when this is necessary, for regeneration is essential to the well-being of any Pisces-influenced person. As a rule, however, this person is a party animal, even if it is one who will often be seen standing in the corner, just listening.

Don't underestimate the power of this type. Intuition allied to action is a formidable combination and when the chips are down, Leo with Pisces Rising is more than willing to take chances. In relationships, the magnetic qualities of Pisces are allied to the charm of Leo in a way that creates a nature positively shouting popularity. Invariably a steadfast partner, Leo with Pisces Rising may not be involved in too many relationships that could be considered serious, except for the one that really counts.

Chapter 19
Rising Signs for Virgo

Virgo with Aries Rising

This is a naturally useful combination since it enhances the potential of Virgo, bringing a much more dynamic personality and overcoming some of the difficulties that often come with Virgo alone. This individual is a deep thinker, and yet a good communicator and someone who knows how to take decisive action when necessary.

Aries complements Virgo on several different levels. Most noticeable is the fact that all those Virgoan ideas can now find a ready outlet to the world at large. Coming to terms with what life actually offers will be easy and can allow the Virgoan imagination to be a conduit for plans that may eventually be fully realised. Since these individuals are naturally at ease with themselves, relationships become less complicated too.

Virgo with Taurus Rising

Both Virgo and Taurus are Earth signs, so we should not expect this combination to produce particularly progressive people. That does not mean there is any lack of potential for success, for Virgo with Taurus Rising is able to get on well in life, sometimes in ways that more dynamic souls would not. Here we have an easy-going nature, which shows a talkative, friendly exterior, overlaying a very deep mind and great intuition. True, this character can sometimes be a little lazy, though when applied fully this is a very useful, practical combination.

It would be rather difficult to dislike this sort of person, which is why Virgo with Taurus Rising usually has many friends. Kind and considerate, this is also a very artistic sort of individual and one who would prefer a comfortable and settled sort of home life. Although not overtly argumentative, Virgo with Taurus Rising can be extremely stubborn and once embarked on a particular course of action will not be diverted or distracted. Many people would say that as a partner or friend this person cannot be bettered. Loyalty is part of the package.

Virgo with Gemini Rising

There is nothing remotely paradoxical about the way this individual deals with life, even though it might appear that this would be the case. The mixture of Earth and Air doesn't always work as well as is the case for Virgo with Gemini Rising, who appears to have all the practicality and common sense of Virgo, whilst at the same time being gregarious, cheerful and able to think on many different levels simultaneously.

Here we have a mischief-maker, though not someone who is overtly devious. There is something deeply comical and attractive about this combination. Capable of personal and practical success, this is one of the manifestations of Virgo that really gets on in life. Mercury rules both signs and that is the clue to the potential locked into this individual.

Virgo with Cancer Rising

Here we find one of the kindest manifestations of the sign of Virgo. People with this combination are genuinely pleasant. They retain the Virgoan ability to talk to almost anyone but are not quite so fussy as the sign of the Virgin can sometimes be. There is a potential depth of love here that may leave many people guessing, plus practical skills that allow this individual to serve society in a very definite way. Rarely impulsive, Virgo with Cancer Rising is, nevertheless, inclined to surprise others frequently.

With plenty of love to spare, this individual was more or less born for deep, personal attachments. The combination is adaptable and will readily change to suit prevailing circumstances. Although strongly intuitive, it tends to manifest this quality in a very practical manner, and usually on behalf of others. These characters gain and maintain a level of popularity that is justified by their altruism. The nature is, however, nervy at base.

Virgo with Leo Rising

Potentially one of the most successful of the Virgo combinations, Leo brings to this nature a magnanimous, almost regal, bearing and lightens the load of Virgo when taken alone. Gains are made in life through careful planning followed by dynamic action. Rarely back-biting or devious, Virgo with Leo Rising is also brave, determined and willing to go to almost any lengths on behalf of friends or loved ones.

This is someone who has great reserves of energy. The basic nature can show nervous tendencies, as is the case with any Virgoan combination. However, here it is controlled and used positively. This character can make money easily and finds great joy in relationships at any level, someone who is never short of something to say and who will usually make friends happy.

Virgo with Virgo Rising

Both good and not-so-good traits of the sign of Virgo are amplified when this combination is present. This person was born at dawn, and that often brings a progressive streak to the nature, allied to the naturally outgoing qualities that Virgo possesses in abundance. The mind is penetrating, though basically introverted, so that verbal contact with the world at large may often seem insincere. However, we have here one of the deepest thinkers imaginable and a person who can gain significantly from putting pen to paper. Double Virgo is a communicator through and through, even if sometimes a fairly repressed one.

Keen to have a tidy and comfortable home, Virgo with Virgo Rising can sometimes appear rather fussy about details and may sulk when things are not going as they would wish. In personal relationships, this person is steadfast and loyal, usually choosing and maintaining only one major relationship in life. The potential for financial success is strong here, though only when double Virgo applies its genuine skills to the full.

Virgo with Libra Rising

Probably the most happy-go-lucky manifestation of Virgo and certainly the combination that is most comfortable in its dealings with the world at large. There is tremendous emotional equilibrium here, though with more genuine depth to the nature than is sometimes the case with Libran contacts. Popularity is almost certain and comes about because this is a person who would go to great lengths to both listen to and assist friends.

Virgo with Libra Rising finds it easy to survive in the real world. A theorist and yet someone who is immensely practical, this type has little difficulty in establishing a comfortable position in life, both professionally and personally. Double-dealing is out of the question, though the nervous system may not be especially strong and it takes constant compliments to make this person truly self-confident.

Virgo with Scorpio Rising

Not the easiest combination for Virgo in terms of the way it communicates with the world at large, though a deep and magnetic individual who will cause people to look twice. Virgo with Scorpio Rising has tremendous latent strength, though of the sort that manifests itself quietly and sometimes subversively. This individual is completely honest, but their opinions are so carefully guarded that their ultimate actions can appear quite baffling and mysterious.

Anyone who can truly get inside this combination will find a loyal and persevering friend who will still be around many years hence. Virgo with

Scorpio Rising doesn't care too much for change, isn't a particularly good traveller and will often stay in the same house for half a lifetime. This combination really does need funny and flippant people around, who lighten the atmosphere and make life more entertaining. Not everyone finds this sort of person easy to get on with and yet, fundamentally, there isn't a more genuine person to be found anywhere.

Virgo with Sagittarius Rising

Although predominantly a very progressive combination, Virgo with Sagittarius Rising manifests itself in a number of divergent and often paradoxical ways. Sagittarius brings a very outgoing personality and an ability for Virgo to make a real impression on the world at large. However, the combination of these two signs can make for a slightly over-fussy attitude and even a sarcastic streak. All too often, petty envies and jealousies are present. These are unnecessary and unworthy of this individual.

This is someone who really does need to play life with a straight bat. Truthfulness and a determination to do well through personal effort are essential, together with steadfast friends, of which there will almost certainly be many. This individual will be an entertaining partner and a solid, if somewhat capricious, friend.

Virgo with Capricorn Rising

These may not be the most entertaining people in the world, but boy, can they get things done! These individuals are constantly beavering away in the background, using good practical skills and excellent observation to increase gradually both influence and success. Virgos with Capricorn Rising aren't especially noisy, though they tend to be friendly and reasonably outgoing. Shyness in youth is soon left behind but arrogance is almost unknown to this combination.

As friends, these types are solid and steadfast, often funny and quite willing to put themselves out for others. However, at base there is a somewhat selfish streak that causes these individuals to feather their own nest, together with those of loved ones and family members.

Maybe not the most progressive person on the planet, but one who always seems to get on and who can easily pull others along with them, Virgo with Capricorn Rising is a good homemaker and also quite adaptable. Ultimate material success is more or less assured with this combination.

Virgo with Aquarius Rising

There is a lightness and brightness in this nature that lifts Virgo to new heights in terms of interest and activity. Here we find someone with great latent power to amuse, who will readily adapt to suit prevailing circumstances. Virgo with Aquarius Rising has a tremendous curiosity and exhibits a friendly, if somewhat quirky, nature that others find instantly appealing.

The motivation here is essentially mental activity, though Virgo brings practical skills and adds to a generally rounded nature that takes life pretty much in its stride. Rarely argumentative, and yet penetrating, this is someone who can genuinely contribute to the well-being of others and who forms positive and lasting relationships. In any group, Virgo with Aquarius Rising tends to be extremely popular.

Virgo with Pisces Rising

Although an extremely pleasant type, Virgo with Pisces Rising isn't especially easy to understand fully. Virgo tends to be talkative, though the presence of Pisces can quieten the nature, and certainly deepens it. The motivation behind its actions is usually noble and this is the sort of individual who would work hard on behalf of the world at large, whilst paying specific attention to the needs of friends and loved ones. A very family-motivated combination, this is someone who genuinely wants to help, but whose quiet ways sometimes get in the way.

On a personal level, this type of Virgoan is steadfast and loyal, though sometimes embarks on romantic entanglements too early in life, leading to problems later. Virgo with Pisces Rising has a latent intuition and a deep attraction that others find difficult to avoid. Getting to know this type isn't easy but when the link is established, there is plenty to fascinate the observer. Whether anyone actually 'knows' the real Virgo with Pisces Rising remains in doubt. This is the most mysterious Virgo type.

Chapter 20
Rising Signs for Libra

Libra with Aries Rising

In this combination we find all the outgoing, cheerful qualities that are normally expected of Libra, together with a slightly more dominant and self-assured overlay. Librans are sometimes accused of being indecisive, but that is not something that is apparent when Aries forms part of the picture.

This is an easy person to deal with in any form of relationship. Although often more outspoken that Libra when taken alone, the nature here is, nevertheless, refined, potentially successful and yet still easy-going. These characters can deal well with rules and regulations and are not easily discouraged. They frequently work on behalf of humanity. On the whole, Librans with Aries Rising are usually very popular and invariably enjoy the stimulation that comes from having many different sorts of friends.

Libra with Taurus Rising

Libra and Taurus do have something very important in common – they are both ruled by the planet Venus. As a result, this individual is naturally settled, cultured, intelligent and kind. There are usually strong artistic inclinations, together with a desire to see the world filled with harmony. Libra with Taurus Rising hates argument and upheaval and may sometimes shy away from situations that it finds unpleasant to look at.

As a friend, this individual is considerate and easy to get on with. Success is a distinct possibility in business, though usually in terms of clean or administrative jobs, since Libra with Taurus Rising is not keen to get its hands dirty. It has an equitable nature that thrives on love and affection. This person is highly unlikely to become involved in deep-seated arguments or contentious issues, preferring a steady life that allows maximum expression of an inner calm. As a life partner, many consider Libra with Taurus Rising to be ideal. At base, however, this type is quite nervy and surroundings are clearly all-important to its well-being.

Libra with Gemini Rising

It is not always easy to differentiate between this sort of Libran and the typical Gemini subject. As a result, we find here a friendly, garrulous, outgoing and even brash sort of individual. Gemini is often accused of being fickle and flighty and of having an over-stimulated nervous system. These are suggestions that fit Libra with Gemini Rising too, because there is a capricious quality that is evident at almost every level. However, there are differences. The strong qualities of Libra make for an individual who has a strong sense of justice and a need for harmony. Libra with Gemini Rising is not as contentious as Gemini, though rather more outspoken than Libra. The combination gives 'bite' to the nature and brings a degree of success greater than either Libra or Gemini taken alone could expect. An easy person to know and like.

Libra with Cancer Rising

This is often thought of as being one of the most pleasant manifestations of Libra, with the presence of the sign of Cancer helping to create a very likeable nature. Although probably quieter than Librans are sometimes inclined to be, this is someone who can be talkative when necessary but who may prefer to sit on the sidelines of life for much of the time.

Libra with Cancer Rising longs for harmony and is particularly protective of family and friends. Change isn't always easily dealt with and a settled home life appears to be particularly important to this combination. If there is a fault here it could be that routine is so important that the possibility of moving forward progressively in life is sometimes not addressed.

These individuals make admirable friends, though they are probably happy with their own company for much of the time. Libra with Cancer Rising is a loving partner and a doting parent, a basically gentle soul and yet practically productive. It is hard to fall out with this likeable individual.

Libra with Leo Rising

This may well be the most progressive type of Libran subject. Leo within the Libran nature means that the naturally balanced tendencies are enhanced and offered a degree of immediacy that is not often present with Libra taken alone. Libra with Leo Rising is capable of fighting tenaciously for the sake of those it loves and it particularly dislikes unfairness or cruelty of any sort.

Whereas Libra is often inclined to take the line of least resistance, or at least sit on the fence, this character is more combative and able to hold its own in almost any sort of conversation. Libra with Leo Rising can easily get on in life. In a career sense, it is the ideal combination to be put in charge of enterprises. From the perspective of love, the combination brings greater constancy and a romantic potential that may well be peerless.

Libra with Virgo Rising

This Libran is probably quite hesitant most of the time and will not be pushed into doing anything that goes against the grain. Its powers of communication are especially good and nobody watching from the outside would ever guess that it is a potential shrinking violet. Even a relatively good friend will be hard put to understand the lack of personal confidence that can lie within this astrological combination, and then only with the passage of time.

All the same, Libra with Virgo Rising has many positive qualities. Benefits can often be found through property, dealings with the law and friends. Family members are important and there is an automatic desire here to build a solid foundation for life on all levels. This is not a contentious type, though it can throw up people who fuss and become excessively nervous when they feel in any way threatened. In all kinds of partnerships, business and personal, this is a person who can be safely trusted.

Libra with Libra Rising

It may appear that no one could fail both to like and to respect the double Libran subject. On the whole, this combination breeds culture, a great sense of harmony, deeply artistic qualities and a love of justice. Double Libra is enthusiastic, a good communicator and a tireless worker for equality. There is nothing at all rude or aggressive in this nature and so it makes very many friends – though always of a particular type – and yet, surprisingly, there are some who will not find this combination to their liking.

Double Libra needs support and encouragement. The adult nature is often deeply influenced by situations that took place early in childhood – this is someone who can rise above adversity but who will always be marked by past events.

In personal relationships, there are potential problems for double Libra, who may not be quite as constant or deeply affectionate as some Libran zodiac sign combinations.

Libra with Scorpio Rising

Scorpio may bring a steadfast quality to Libra that it sometimes lacks when taken alone. Certainly we find here someone who is likely to be rather quieter than the average Libran individual, someone who is thoughtful, considerate and quite hard to fathom. Friendship is very important to this person and is never taken lightly; there is a steadfast intention to support both relatives and friends alike. It is likely that Libra with Scorpio Rising will be able to build a sound financial base and can be relied upon to work long and hard to achieve its objectives.

Really getting inside this person is difficult – as with any zodiac combination that involves the sign of Scorpio – though persistence will pay dividends. Although absolute self-confidence may be in short supply, it can be encouraged and strengthened with the passing of time. Emotionally, Libra with Scorpio Rising is settled and takes well to deep and lasting relationships. Be warned, however: this combination can fight.

Libra with Sagittarius Rising

It would be hard to miss this character, even in a crowd. Cheerful, easy to get to know and very committed to life in general, Libra with Sagittarius Rising is a natural communicator and loves the cut and thrust of life. There is a certain likeable eccentricity about this combination that makes it even more attractive than might otherwise be the case, together with a magnetic personality and a good balance between thought and action.

Sometimes considered flighty, Libra with Sagittarius Rising has, nevertheless, great potential for success in business, and is possessed of a shrewd understanding of people. Although generally popular, this combination is not everyone's cup of tea and might be seen as being slightly odd by some. Libra with Sagittarius Rising sometimes has problems maintaining personal relationships over long periods of time.

Libra with Capricorn Rising

In this combination we find Libran affability allied to a practical and determined core. Capricorn, though generally a quiet zodiac sign, knows how to get things done. As a result, this is not a combination that creates fence-sitters of the typical Libran sort. On the contrary, Libra with Capricorn Rising brings the more positive qualities within the sign of the Scales to the surface. Practical matters especially are dealt with easily and well by this person.

Relationships are less of a problem with this zodiac combination than may be the case for Libra when taken alone. The presence of the sign of the Goat allows this type to think more deeply and to establish a firmer base, particularly with regard to marriage and home life. Routines are no problem to this type and neither is the application of effort over a long period of time. In the end, success is almost inevitable and manifests itself in many different areas of life.

Libra with Aquarius Rising

Perhaps one of the oddest and yet the most potentially attractive of the Libran combinations, Libra with Aquarius Rising is unique in almost every way. Instinctive, filled with intuitive foresight and quite charismatic, this is someone who should find it easy to get on in life, especially when it comes to its associations with other people. Libra with Aquarius Rising is rarely stuck for something to say and is usually listened to avidly.

Although this may not be the best combination for success in long-term relationships, with time and experience Libra with Aquarius Rising does usually settle down and will often find its greatest happiness in the middle years of life. Commitment towards family is less well accented here, but present nevertheless.

Libra with Pisces Rising

By no means an extrovert, Libra with Pisces Rising is, all the same, friendly, easy to talk to and essentially very kind. It would be very hard to dislike this personality, though there is certainly more to it than meets the eye. This is the combination of Libra that probably does the most for humanity as a whole, and because it cares about everyone, relatives, friends and even romantic partners may find themselves losing out on occasions.

There is a sort of idealism here that is always present in Libra, but which shows itself particularly clearly in this pairing. There can be no doubting the basic good intentions of Libra with Pisces Rising, even if the motivating forces lie so deep within the individual that they are hard to locate. The intentions of these people are never in doubt. The combination possesses a practical ability, though is sometimes inclined to shy away from a reality that it doesn't care to address. Libra with Pisces Rising is complex and difficult to understand fully, and sometimes appears over-emotional.

Chapter 21
Rising Signs for Scorpio

Scorpio with Aries Rising

In general, Scorpio with Aries Rising strengthens the Scorpio nature considerably, making the individual more likely to speak out on issues that are important, and also emphasising the ability to think and act more quickly. They may tend to be sarcastic, and this is a personality that should not be crossed by the faint-hearted.

Here we find someone who is occasionally given to impulsive actions but who, under most circumstances, is apt to be quiet and sometimes to even stay in the shadows. Not easy to understand, this individual can prove to be audacious and very brave when necessary. Extremely supportive of family, friends and loved ones, Scorpio with Aries Rising has magnetism of a quiet sort and is capable of great insights.

Scorpio with Taurus Rising

With this combination, we find someone capable of great reserve but who approaches the world in a generally friendly manner. Taurus brings a greater gentleness to Scorpio and may help to curb the occasional rash or impetuous behaviour. The presence of the sign of the Bull here does add to the stubborn qualities of the individual; for example, there is no point in trying to make this person do anything at all against their will.

Generally loving and kind, like all Scorpios, this example is fond of anyone with whom it feels a bond of friendship, kinship or romance. Steadfast and loyal under almost all conditions, they would fight tenaciously when roused, but, under normal circumstances, would rather remain in the background. There can be traces of Scorpio jealousy if provoked, though in the main this type of Scorpion will be happy to settle for a relatively quiet life. Family relationships are especially important and younger family members are particularly cherished. As with all Scorpios, this person is not easy to understand but does respond extremely well to kindness and will always return a favour tenfold.

Scorpio with Gemini Rising

This is an unusual mixture between two signs that don't appear to have too much in common. A talkative and outgoing Scorpio seems to be a contradiction in terms, which is why it is difficult to know exactly how to take this type. Although usually friendly and approachable, Scorpio with Gemini Rising can sometimes exhibit a somewhat caustic attitude and is impossible to better in open discussion. Only the most intuitive of friends will be able to sum up what makes this person tick but the combination brings loyalty and a tremendous desire and ability to speak out for the downtrodden or those who have no voice of their own.

Scorpio with Gemini Rising feels the same sort of commitment to friends and loved ones as any individual ruled by Scorpio but has the capacity to express this concern in a more tangible manner. The very act of giving voice to its feelings and emotions may somehow diffuse a few of the less positive qualities of what is an essentially repressed zodiac sign, and may also offer a refreshing look into the heart of unusual Scorpio.

Scorpio with Cancer Rising

Cancer joins well with Scorpio, bringing about the sort of individual who appears to be rounded, contented and generally settled. This person is certainly not gregarious and may be extremely quiet by nature. Nevertheless there is a latent power that will become obvious if the sign combination is threatened or is sticking up for those it loves. Other people may feel that it is possible to browbeat this person, but they are likely to receive a distinct shock if they try.

Extremely aware of social and personal responsibilities, Scorpio with Cancer Rising works very hard and seeks to put right wrongs and to offer assistance when it is needed. Almost invariably, this combination works on behalf of humanity as a whole, often in one of the caring professions.

Scorpio with Leo Rising

This is the combination of a social reformer. Scorpio and Leo appear to be very different but they have one thing in common – they are both very brave. As a result, we find the social conscience of Scorpio allied to the reforming zeal that it brings to Leo. Not everyone is going to care for this character, but it would be hard to criticise the motivation or the resultant actions.

Scorpio with Leo Rising is not nearly as quiet as Scorpio when taken alone and always seems to be involved in some sort of quest. It is possible for friends to break this cycle of good causes and when this happens we find a person who is quite able to enjoy life to the full. As a friend or a romantic partner, Scorpio with Leo Rising may seem ideal. Under all but the most extreme circumstances this is true, but beware a desire on rare occasions to own rather than to help loved ones.

Scorpio with Virgo Rising

This can be a dark and gloomy combination in some cases, unless the person concerned has learned how to turn their mind outwards towards the world at large. Sometimes inclined to look on the black side of life, Scorpio with Virgo Rising needs constant stimulation and support from much more cheerful types. As a friend, this individual is loyal to the bitter end and can actually be very funny sometimes.

This is a zodiac combination that can lavish attention on those it loves and especially on a prospective romantic partner. Constancy is part of the package, though there may be a slight lack of imagination when it comes to showing love in an open sense. It would be extremely hard to dislike this type of person but friends could sometimes find it difficult to be sure that they have genuinely made contact. An open, free-thinking and excitement-loving attitude needs to be engendered if at all possible.

Scorpio with Libra Rising

This is the friendly face of Scorpio, made very much more approachable with the addition of Libra, a zodiac sign that offers a lighter touch to the Scorpion and the chance for it to make real contact with the world at large. There is certainly depth to this nature and an insatiable desire to put things right, particularly for people who have no voice of their own. The jealous side of Scorpio is less inclined to show with Libra present and the approach to the world is affable, though generally quiet.

Getting on with the job in hand is quite easy for Scorpio with Libra Rising, which also demonstrates a great desire to love and to be loved. With openness of attitude, a genuine desire to be involved and yet a sort of reserve, this is someone who makes a staunch ally, a good friend and possibly a perfect partner.

Scorpio with Scorpio Rising

Every trait generally expected of the Scorpion is on offer here. Double Scorpio is dark, secretive, quiet and inclined to flare up suddenly if provoked. This is the side of the sign that many people don't like but there is another, much more likeable, Scorpio on offer. If a capacity to love deeply is one of the greatest blessings nature can bestow upon an individual, then this Scorpio is well blessed indeed. There isn't a more loyal friend or a more committed romantic partner than double Scorpio, as many people in the world can surely testify.

Beware the typical Scorpio jealousy on occasions. This stems from a lack of personal confidence and a certainty that there are more worthy types around. Double Scorpio is not at all confident in its own ability to be lovable. Some time spent in a truly settled relationship should cause this individual to settle and to begin to exhibit the many rare and wonderful qualities that Scorpio people as a whole possess. Amongst these is a deep and abiding warmth.

Scorpio with Sagittarius Rising

This is a somewhat strange combination because it tends to lead to an animated Scorpion, which, except under fairly exceptional circumstances, isn't normal. Sagittarius here enlivens the nature, though it may not make it very much more outgoing in a conversational sense. More likely, it will contribute to bringing about individuals who pit themselves against a series of personal challenges and who relish physical hardship as a means of promoting better self-understanding.

Some, but not all, people from this combination will favour the Sagittarian aspect, in which case an open, friendly and sociable Scorpio displays itself to the world at large. At heart, however, the sign of the Archer does not usually swamp the basic Scorpio tendencies. As a result, there is the depth in this combination that one would expect of Scorpio.

Scorpio with Capricorn Rising

Capricorn sits well with Scorpio, as it does with many zodiac signs. Often Scorpio wishes it could do more in a practical sense for those it loves, and for the world at large. The presence of Capricorn as the Rising Sign makes this possible. Probably the hardest of Scorpio workers, this person will put in any amount of effort to get a result. Beavering away, quietly and often behind the scenes, this is someone who can make a great deal of difference and who will never be thwarted once they have decided on a particular course of action.

Although deeply committed to those it loves, Scorpio with Capricorn Rising may be less inclined to verbalise its feelings, making it difficult for the recipients of its affection to realise what is going on. Greater freedom of expression is required and this comes when the sign combination is willing to mix with, and be influenced by, more gregarious types. Nevertheless, this is a loyal and warm partner and a staunch friend. Family concerns are uppermost in the mind of the Capricorn Scorpio.

Scorpio with Aquarius Rising

The presence of Aquarius can be a real boon to the average Scorpio type. Aquarius can be a distinctly odd sign but it works well in tandem with the reserved Scorpio tendencies. Certainly, it goes towards creating an eccentric nature but one that is refreshing, original and much admired by others.

Scorpios who have Aquarius Rising should never try to curb their originality. They tend to be far more verbal than Scorpio taken alone and will often work furiously to support people or causes that are important to them. Having little or no Scorpio jealousy, this type of person is capable of forming happy and long-lasting relationships. Even on the level of friendship, it isn't unusual to find it in lifelong attachments.

Scorpio with Pisces Rising

This individual may be inhibited by the fact that neither Scorpio nor Pisces is a particularly gregarious sign. As a result, no matter what is on offer, displaying it in the shop window of personality isn't going to be especially easy. Of course, Pisces is approachable, friendly and kind and, when allied to the strength of Scorpio, it produces a person who cares deeply about others and who tries desperately to find ways to display the concern. There is great innate strength but this usually shows only when Scorpio with Pisces Rising is pushed into a testing situation.

This may be one of the most likeable individuals around, though being so hard to recognise, the sheer beauty of this combination is rarely appreciated to the full. To achieve such recognition requires better powers of communication and greater confidence. This begins when Scorpio with Pisces Rising understands how much it has going for it. The combination makes for a loyal family member and a romantic partner of the best kind. There is also a very strong commitment to children. Deep friendships may be less common once Scorpio with Pisces Rising commits itself romantically.

Chapter 22
Rising Signs for Sagittarius

Sagittarius with Aries Rising

Sagittarius with Aries Rising is one of the most potent of all astrological combinations. Here we have the dynamism of two Fire signs presented to the world within the same individual. Progressive, bright, adventurous and sometimes domineering, these individuals know what they want and are prepared to go to great lengths to get it. It has to be said from the start that not everyone will care for these types, but they certainly cannot be ignored.

Sagittarius brings to this party a more magnetic personality and the ability to use the many skills of Aries to the full. In terms of relationships, this is a person who will make a good friend and who is definitely looking for excitement. There is hardly a dull moment when Sagittarius with Aries Rising is on the scene and whatever the relationship is, excitement abounds.

Sagittarius with Taurus Rising

Here we have the sunny, outgoing and positive qualities of the Archer, allied to the more practical abilities and more artistic refinement of the Bull. Sagittarius with Taurus Rising indicates a nature that is anxious to please and finds many and varied ways of doing so. Charming, fond of creating new and interesting diversions and always up for a laugh – that's the sort of person who is born under this combination. Encapsulated within this individual is the potential for personal and friendship success.

When taken alone, Sagittarius is sometimes accused of being a fairly shallow zodiac sign. The presence of Taurus in the mix strengthens the loyalty and creates a character who finds holding on to deep attachments that much easier. A settled home life is usually forthcoming and multiple marriages are far less likely for this type of Sagittarian than will be the case when the sign mixes with other zodiac types. Despite all this, this is a person who desires material success.

Sagittarius with Gemini Rising

This person is a genuine 'character' and not likely to be forgotten the minute they leave a room. In the astrological world, Gemini and Sagittarius are probably the two most outgoing zodiac signs. They are opposites on the astrological wheel, yet they display themselves to the world at large in very much the same way. Both are inspirational, extremely communicative and full of ingenious ideas but they may lack constancy.

There are many words that could be used to describe this individual, though 'deep' would hardly be one of them. We see in this combination a person who likes to have fun, and is certainly not a born philosopher. It is within this light-hearted approach that the most enjoyable qualities of Sagittarius and Gemini can be appreciated.

Sagittarius with Cancer Rising

This combination is apt to be typical of Sagittarius, though with a less fickle nature and a greater sense of conscience. In terms of deep attachments, many would find it to be the best Sagittarian combination of them all. This manifestation of the sign of the Archer generally loses nothing in terms of overall character, being easy-going, hard-hitting and usually quite successful in life. But there is a degree of depth and a desire to spend at least part of life thinking about and working on behalf of others.

Sagittarius with Cancer Rising tends to bring about individuals who have a high regard for friendship and who show a deeper loyalty than is often evident in Sagittarius alone. Kind, considerate, accommodating and yet still strong, this combination also has an in-built desire to explore the world and a fondness for travel that invariably finds some sort of outlet. Not a character who will be restricted in any way and someone who finds joy in almost every aspect of life.

Sagittarius with Leo Rising

This is another of the double Fire-sign combinations, but it manifests itself slightly differently than would Sagittarius with Aries Rising. There is a strong sense of material awareness and a desire to get on in life, but allied to these are the more regal qualities that Leo brings to bear on the mix. Fond of fun, happy to be the leader in almost any situation and very gregarious, Sagittarius with Leo Rising also insists on having many causes to work for, at least some of which aim to improve the environment and the lives of other people.

In terms of its interreaction with others, this type is a very loyal friend and someone who makes practical suggestions. Although they may not look at life too deeply, there is a natural desire for some kind of stability and plenty of commitment to personal attachments and family issues.

Sagittarius with Virgo Rising

The most noticeable effect when Virgo is brought to bear on the sign of Sagittarius is that the individual concerned is tidier and more methodical than might otherwise be expected. Virgo brings a more contemplative tone to the ever-gregarious and fairly superficial Archer, and also deepens its communication skills. This is a combination often possessed by politicians – and Sagittarius with Virgo Rising is not against making U-turns, if necessary.

Always alert, sometimes nervy but generally very easy to get along with, this combination may display a slight tendency to backbiting, which could have a bearing on friendships. Overall, this is someone who is quite willing to commit to long-term relationships, but usually only after a fairly protracted period during which the individuals concerned come to understand themselves first. These types are frequently financially successful.

Sagittarius with Libra Rising

It would almost be impossible to dislike these individuals. Sagittarius with Libra Rising is extremely talkative, able to look at life in a very positive manner and yet tries constantly to see the other person's point of view and to do the right thing by others. Creative, inspirational and often extremely witty, they are great to have at parties and to talk to late into the night.

This is a person who always has something new to say and who would rarely if ever be seen as boring. Their natural zest for life can be slightly wearing, but fortunately it is allied to a deeper and more contemplative quality, so there are bound to be times when Sagittarius with Libra Rising will sit and listen. All in all, this is an immensely likeable person, though not one who wants to rule the world.

Sagittarius with Scorpio Rising

This is an unusual mixture. Like oil and water, Sagittarius and Scorpio don't have a great deal in common and so rarely create a comfortable chemistry. What generally happens is that parts of the nature respond to the Sun Sign and other components to the Rising Sign. Often outgoing and gregarious, this individual has a very deep core, which doesn't show itself in everyday life and certainly not in amongst the cut and thrust of professional situations.

Although this person is generally a good talker, there is a deeply philosophical streak and an inner wisdom that has to be teased out carefully. Paradoxical, unusual and sometimes a little caustic, Scorpio offers the hardest Sagittarian Rising Sign combination to understand but is well worth the time needed to do so.

Sagittarius with Sagittarius Rising

If you need someone to sell refrigerators to Eskimos, look no further than Sagittarius with Sagittarius Rising. Life is a roller-coaster ride when in the company of this type. Irrepressible, quick, witty, dominant and yet utterly charming, double Sagittarius has a good understanding of life on a superficial level and probably doesn't want to plumb the depths in any case.

This individual may be the very best friend imaginable, at least as long as that is what they want. Don't expect a great deal in the way of constancy, however. This is someone who bores easily and who will only play the game by their own rules. Double Sagittarius will be either rich or a pauper, either totally committed to relationships or searching for new ones. There are absolutely no half measures here.

Sagittarius with Capricorn Rising

Here we find all the zest, love of life and talkative qualities of Sagittarius, allied to the down-to-earth and practical Capricorn. The resulting mixture may prove more successful than either of its components and in terms of living life on a day-to-day level, the Sagittarian with Capricorn Rising exhibits little difficulty. Jobs get done in a flash, whilst understanding of the necessities of life is instinctive to this pairing. Thought and application come together better in this combination than in almost any other zodiac sign mix.

This individual is friendly, committed and far less shallow than Sagittarius when taken alone, and has a disposition that is very easy both to understand and to deal with. Although a seasoned debater and a truly social animal, Sagittarius with Capricorn Rising can be steadfast, loyal and true to genuine convictions. This may be the most noble of all the possible Sagittarian combinations. The only small fly in the ointment is a slight tendency towards bouts of exhaustion.

Sagittarius with Aquarius Rising

Another very promising coming-together, though far less practical than Sagittarius with Capricorn Rising, inheriting instead a truly inspirational quality, but losing out on constancy and staying-power. Sagittarius with Aquarius Rising creates people of great magnetism and charm, though this is sometimes allied to deep eccentricity. This individual is a genuine one-off and not someone who would readily give in to convention at any level. Look out for deep intuition and lightning-quick thought processes.

They may or may not make an ideal friend or even marital partner – it really depends on the two people involved. To some, this person will be all fascination, whilst others may feel that there is a great deal of interesting froth on this beer, but very little liquid. This is someone who loves to have fun and who wants to share the world with everyone else. Following the peculiar reasoning processes inherent in this nature isn't too easy.

Sagittarius with Pisces Rising

This is the quietest type of Sagittarian, but maybe one of the most sincere. Although still given to being gregarious, Sagittarius with Pisces Rising is liable to be contemplative on occasions. Much of the power of the sign of the Archer is here given over to service to others, because no contact involving Pisces can possibly avoid it. There is compassion, sensitivity and depth, though all are expressed through the positive characteristics that the Archer typifies.

In personal attachments, this is a Sagittarian who 'sticks'. Deep attachments mean a great deal to this sort of Archer, who is likely to take on lifelong relationships and will derive a great deal of pleasure from both understanding and nurturing. In Sagittarius with Pisces Rising you will find a staunch and loyal friend, a caring relative and a loving partner. Also in the mix is a healthy sense of humour and a curiosity that is truly infectious.

Chapter 23
Rising Signs for Capricorn

Capricorn with Aries Rising

This is a fortunate combination for the sign of Capricorn, though one that tends to swamp some of the quieter, more contemplative aspects of the sign of the Goat. Here we find an individual who is far more progressive and inclined to push forward in leaps and bounds. Where the balance is right, Capricorn with Aries Rising demonstrates the application of practical skills, whilst harnessing the differing energies of both the zodiac signs involved.

In terms of relationships, this species of Capricorn is more inclined to get involved in a big way. Powers of communication are better than they are with Capricorn taken alone and the nature is supportive, direct and fairly methodical. Though not always considered a particularly warm person, Capricorn with Aries Rising does fulfil all its obligations to family, friends and romantic partners alike.

Capricorn with Taurus Rising

This is a combination in which two Earth signs come together to form a cohesive and generally successful nature. Although not at all a noisy person, Capricorn with Taurus Rising can get its message across. There are strong artistic qualities and probably a good deal of creative potential, which manifests itself in practical ways. This person will want and respect tidy and happy surroundings. They will also be open to suggestions, as long as these are fair.

What this combination will not stand for is being told what to do. Both of these zodiac signs are known as being potentially stubborn and when they come together, the chances of moving the result by brute force are practically nil. There is strong and enduring commitment to family and friends, plus a deep and abiding loyalty and much practical support. Many people will consider this type to be an ideal partner, if only because of the constancy that is engendered by this combination. Capricorn with Taurus Rising can seem old-fashioned but is none the worse for that.

Capricorn with Gemini Rising

Capricorn with Gemini Rising can lead to some very useful outcomes in the world at large, bringing, as it does, practicality allied with imagination and flexibility. The two signs tend to ally themselves very well, since each has something very useful to bring to the party. Gemini has a good ability to think up new ideas and to communicate these to others. Where it sometimes falls down is in actually carrying out what it promises. Capricorn in the mix assists this situation enormously, however, and leads to a much more rounded individual than could be expected from either sign alone.

The loyalty of Capricorn, allied to the winning ways of the Gemini, usually makes for a high level of popularity. Potential success is writ large here, together with a friendly and sociable disposition and a strong potential for teamwork. This is not an argumentative person, nor one who is likely to become stuck in any sort of rut.

Capricorn with Gemini Rising is caring and responsible.

Capricorn with Cancer Rising

These zodiac signs are known as astrological opposites and as a result there are both gains and losses in the mix. Certainly, it is sometimes suggested that Capricorn lacks warmth and is fairly clinical and overly practical in its attitude to life. Having the Rising Sign in Cancer tends to modify the nature, however, bringing a greater degree of understanding and heightening the emotional responses a good deal. This in turn creates an individual who is easier to understand and who is responsive to the needs of the world as a whole, and to loved ones especially.

Capricorn with Cancer Rising is not usually a pushy individual and will work long and hard in the background, achieving a great deal and usually forging a large amount of ultimate personal success. Whilst this is also true of Capricorn taken alone, the combination means that much of the effort is given over to support for others. There is strong compassion here and the potential for deep and abiding love.

Capricorn with Leo Rising

Despite lacking much emotional understanding, this is one of the very best astrological mixes for the sign of Capricorn. Leo brings greater determination, a more outgoing personality and certainly much apparent warmth to the nature. Capricorn's ability to work hard and plan ahead remains intact, whilst Leo allows a stronger sense of self-worth and better communication skills.

As already mentioned, if there is anything at all lacking in this mix it might be that the emotions either are suppressed, or else do not run especially deep in the first place. This can lead to an occasional lack of empathy and to a somewhat sterile view of love but this nature does not lack either loyalty or staying-power in personal attachments.

Capricorn with Virgo Rising

This combination can certainly get things done and shows to the world at large probably the most practical face that could be expected of any individual. The presence of Virgo makes Capricorn more inclined to speak out, though it can also add to a slightly fussy attitude that not everyone will like. On the whole, the nature is subdued and perhaps rather too defensive on occasions, though this individual should be able to match up to any expectation that it or the world may hold.

Staunchly defensive of friends, relatives and loved ones generally, Capricorn with Virgo Rising may prove to be the ideal life partner, especially for someone to whom constancy is all-important. There may be a slight lack of imagination and though the nature is inclined to nervous fluctuations, it isn't especially swamped by emotional responses. What can be expected is eventual wealth, through a willingness to work hard and long to achieve objectives. This person is capable, though probably not exciting.

Capricorn with Libra Rising

Capricorn has much to offer the world at large but sometimes fails to demonstrate this directly. In other words, it is necessary to get to know the average person born under the sign of the Goat very well before their true worth can be appreciated. With Libra present, the process is made much easier and the result is greater understanding and happiness all round.

Libra allows Capricorn a way into the hearts and minds of almost anyone. This is a fair nature, balanced and kind. Though losing none of the practical application of Capricorn, this person is able to cut through red tape and to climb high in life. Most importantly, there is a combination of both fundamental and executive skills. This is a good person to know and someone who can be tremendously supportive.

Capricorn with Scorpio Rising

The very depth and accessibility of this astrological pairing may sometimes prevent the world at large from ever getting to know just how emotional, sensitive and caring this person actually is. Capricorn with Scorpio Rising is strongly intuitive, and has an instinctive ability to help those around it. There are strong reforming tendencies here, even if they manifest themselves in generally subdued ways.

A capacity for deep and abiding love is the hallmark of this mix, together with a few of the less endearing qualities of Scorpio that can manifest themselves as jealousy. Being loved by this person can bring a great sense of security, but it can also be somewhat overwhelming. Capricorn with Scorpio Rising is definitely a homemaker and will go to great lengths to prove its attachment, but it is hardly likely to be the most exciting combination within the zodiac as a whole.

Capricorn with Sagittarius Rising

Whenever Capricorn is allied to a much more dynamic and outgoing zodiac sign, the result is likely to seem both interesting and rewarding. This is what happens when it is conjoined with the zodiac sign of the Archer. True, this is not an overly deep person, and there is a certain superficial quality that not everyone will care for. Nevertheless, we have here someone who improves with acquaintance and who proves to be far more approachable than turns out to be the case for Capricorn taken alone.

Capricorn with Sagittarius Rising wants to have fun and is capable of setting the world alight on occasions. All the same, there is an essential reserve here, which shows through quiet personal ways and a fondness for home and family. This is someone who can show great affection but who can sometimes also appear a little cold and detached.

Capricorn with Capricorn Rising

There is absolutely no doubt about what to expect with double Capricorn individuals, because they typify everything that is represented by the sign of the Goat. Careful, attentive to detail and willing to work hard for long periods, double Capricorn knows that success comes through applied effort. Here we find the most loyal Earth sign of them all, though we should not expect eloquent expression of emotions, despite the fact that they are clearly present. Double Capricorn is not given to outbursts of any sort, though it is capable of being very stubborn.

Although somewhat misunderstood, Capricorn people are usually well liked. At worst, they are the back-room boys of life, avoiding fuss and preferring to work on slowly and steadily towards their objectives. Any potential relationship with this individual is hardly likely to be exciting, but many people will be happy with it. Kindness will be present, together with strong support at a practical level.

Capricorn with Aquarius Rising

Aquarius sits well with the basic Capricorn nature, though it is inclined to change it a great deal. This person is apt to be quite original and thinks in very unusual ways. As a result, we discover all sorts of things about the Capricorn nature that are often kept under wraps. Outgoing, interested and always curious, Capricorn with Aquarius Rising wants to be of assistance and usually shows a very intelligent attitude towards life in general. It looks favourably on a range of different sorts of friends and will never allow itself to be typecast.

This might be one of the best Capricorn types in terms of relationships, particularly at a superficial level. Capricorn with Aquarius Rising wants to be out there in the centre of life, even if it sometimes feels vulnerable. Very supportive of friends, though perhaps slightly less so of family, this is someone who views deeper attachments with some suspicion, but who is fun to be around.

Capricorn with Pisces Rising

The whole world would love this person, if it could only get to know it well – but that's not easy. Neither of these signs is a natural communicator, especially at a superficial level. Nevertheless, the presence of Pisces in this mix does afford deep compassion, an ability to attract others in an almost magnetic way and stronger intuitive powers than Capricorn generally possesses. There are also strong tendencies towards nurturing, which often manifest themselves in the choice of profession.

Capricorn with Pisces Rising is full of give and take, since some of the stubborn qualities of the Goat are mitigated in this combination. Commitment to relationships is total, though deeper attachments may take some time to get going. Once the heart of this individual is set on something or someone, it rarely changes. This is not the most brash or outgoing face of Capricorn, but it is kind, sincere, understanding, warm and compassionate.

Chapter 24
Rising Signs for Aquarius

Aquarius with Aries Rising

The essential nature of Aquarius is preserved in this combination, and given an extra boost, thanks to the progressive characteristics of the zodiac sign of Aries. Few would doubt the capable qualities of this individual, who generally manages to get through life with little difficulty and who may also be stronger mentally than Aquarius alone.

Aquarius with Aries Rising is happy, articulate, optimistic and generally above average in terms of intelligence. Although rarely inclined to stay still for long, this individual is a good friend, a positive influence on the world at large and someone who is deeply curious to know what makes the world tick. Relationships are treated seriously, though the resources of Aquarius may be somewhat reduced by the presence of the sign of the Ram. It would be quite hard to dislike this character, though there is something quite forceful about the personality.

Aquarius with Taurus Rising

A quiet Aquarian is almost unheard-of, so even the slightly more laid-back qualities of Taurus are not really going to silence this type. Aquarius with Taurus Rising is generally very creative and may show a definite penchant for fine art and for having a home that is more organised than Aquarians usually worry about. It also has a greater potential for thought allied to action.

This is one of the best combinations for friendship, and perhaps also for deeper relationships. Aquarius, being an Air sign, is not known for its constancy, though there is, in this coming-together, a potential for a desire to settle down. None of the usual inquisitive qualities are missing and, if anything, they tend to be heightened with Taurus as part of the scenario. The loving and nurturing qualities of the sign of the Bull sit well with the more airy and superficial tendencies that are latent here.

Aquarius with Gemini Rising

Up with the lark and on the go from morning until night – that's Aquarius with Gemini Rising. It is hard to conceive of a more curious, fascinating, magnetic or naturally likeable soul than this. Sometimes accused of being fairly shallow, an accusation that really isn't fair, this character is much deeper and certainly more intuitive than most people ever realise. The nature is very busy and if situations or people do get forgotten, it is not with any malice aforethought. Not everyone likes this type, however, though if this is the case an element of jealousy may be part of the reason.

A tireless investigator, Aquarius with Gemini Rising wants to know the ins and outs of every situation. It has excellent communication skills and good executive ability, but may have little time for relationships. Happiness is possible, though only if the potential partner is equally content to be perpetually on the go.

Aquarius with Cancer Rising

This is a fascinating individual, difficult to understand and yet usually happy. It does not set out deliberately to be complicated. On the contrary, Aquarius with Cancer Rising has a strong social nature, a great love of humanity and every shred of the natural charm that is shot through Aquarius. This is someone who actively wants to make others happy and who would willingly work hard to build a secure home.

With a tendency towards romance, this sort of Aquarian knows how to think up and say exactly the right words to sweep someone off their feet. In terms of relationships as a whole, this is a very fortunate combination and is particularly supportive in family settings. This type has a busy mind, but is also possessed of a quieter inner core. Accessible, and willing to discuss most matters, Aquarius with Cancer Rising is certainly not hard to live with.

Aquarius with Leo Rising

This is Aquarius with a regal bearing and with all the pride that the sign of Leo can muster. From the beginning, it will be obvious that this is a powerful individual and certainly not one to be deliberately crossed. Noble, magnanimous, occasionally overbearing but always interesting, this person wants to know as much as possible about life and people, but they can become exhausted with the effort. Although not automatically loved by everyone, Aquarius with Leo Rising is sure to have its admirers at every level.

It can be hard to live with a paragon of virtue, and that is what this individual can sometimes seem to be. This type is more than willing to support friends, family and partner to the absolute full. Never boring and always on the go, Aquarius with Leo Rising is fascinating to most people.

Aquarius with Virgo Rising

One of the accusations levelled at Aquarius, like all of the Air signs, is that it lacks continuity and fails to go into matters with the right level of commitment. This is less of a problem when Virgo is part of the mix because the sign of the Virgin brings better powers of concentration and an ability to see things through to the end, sometimes even in the face of adversity.

Anyone who is prepared to speak up publicly is bound to attract a degree of criticism. This is certainly true of Aquarius with Virgo Rising and so this person doesn't always live an entirely peaceful life. Keen to see society running properly, they usually demonstrate a commitment to social causes. Despite this, there is also generally a desire for a quiet home life and a willingness to adapt to suit prevailing circumstances. Not everyone loves this type, but the majority will respect it. Beware a slightly contentious and even argumentative streak, however.

Aquarius with Libra Rising

Aquarius always manages to put on an especially rewarding show when it is allied to other Air signs, such as Libra. What shines out more than anything in this combination is a desire for fairness and equality. Utterly without any sort of class-consciousness, though often living a very middle-class sort of life, Aquarius with Libra Rising breeds intelligent types, the majority of whom are committed, in one way or another, to the betterment of society.

In personal relationships, this is someone who can seem somewhat superficial and who may not show tremendous commitment in any one specific direction. There is no lack of friendly banter but emotional responses may not be particularly deep. Keep things light and interesting if you are looking for success when allied to this character.

Aquarius with Scorpio Rising

Not the easiest person in the world to understand, Aquarius with Scorpio Rising does gain in terms of emotional stability and constancy. Here we find a nature that is as bright and magnetic on the surface as Aquarius is meant to be, though anyone with the slightest perception will soon realise that this well is extremely deep. Whilst most Aquarians will change their views as readily as their socks, such is not the case when Scorpio is brought to bear on the sign.

Deeply committed to home and family, this is a combination that often inclines to early and happy marriage. Not that being settled personally convinces this person to spend hours sitting in a chair. On the contrary, a sense of personal security will encourage this type to try that much harder to help those around it. If Scorpio restricts the Aquarian nature in any way, it does so positively. There is an innate quietness here that allows the individual to reflect on life far better than Aquarius alone could ever manage. This may be one of the most likeable Aquarians of them all.

Aquarius with Sagittarius Rising

In terms of personal success, especially at a material level, Aquarius with Sagittarius Rising really has it all. Talkative, capable, a natural leader and full of wonderful ideas, here we have someone who can really get on in life, and who attracts others as a magnet attracts iron filings. Almost nobody is immune to this character's charms, which are obvious at every level and from an extremely early age. Aquarius with Sagittarius Rising has a love of life that cannot be repressed and a first-class desire to achieve.

Although heaps of blessings fall upon this combination, it does not breed people who are ideally suited to a conventional type of life or relationship. Those allied to this individual will need to understand that they play a supporting role and that giving in an emotional sense is not all that easy for a person born of this combination.

Aquarius with Capricorn Rising

This is Aquarius with at least one foot nailed to the ground. Some would say this is a good thing, because it allows this unusual, eccentric and deeply fascinating sign to get something done in a concrete sense. All the same, it does also place certain limitations on the nature, most of them inspired by Capricorn's quieter and more practical ways. In the end, the balance may prove to be favourable because we find in this combination someone who has original ideas, allied to sufficient staying-power to put them into action.

Aquarius with Capricorn Rising makes many friends, and though it can be pensive, it is usually to be found in the cut and thrust of social discourse. It puts a great deal of energy into creating comfortable working conditions and has plenty of initiative for getting on. However, this type doesn't want to make its life journey alone. Capricorn offers the incentives to form more permanent attachments than Aquarius might.

Aquarius with Aquarius Rising

The double Aquarian is a magnetic and deeply fascinating sort of individual. This is the sign of the zodiac that rules all new innovations and original thought. Absolutely modern, though at the same time quirky and hard to classify, double Aquarius supplies a fountain of fascination that would satisfy almost anyone for a lifetime.

Actually understanding what makes this person tick is probably impossible. That's because the nature changes from one moment to the next. What does remain intact is the friendly manner, the classless approach to life and the insatiable desire simply to know what's going on. Double Aquarians often form unconventional relationships but have so much to offer that others are invariably willing to co-operate.

Aquarius with Pisces Rising

Aquarius and Pisces are two zodiac signs that may not mix too readily, tending rather to create an individual who shows a leaning to either zodiac sign, depending on the circumstances. Certainly Aquarius's energies may be slowed down, or redirected, with Pisces about, and it may often become more of a social reformer, rather than just a reporter on life. It deals more easily with routines and the general level of patience tends to be increased in the case of this combination.

Commitment towards family and friends is not likely to be in doubt. Pisces cares deeply for its nearest and dearest, whilst Aquarius allows these attachments to be handled in an unconventional but generally refreshing way. There is something slightly odd about this zodiac combination, but that may only provide a deeper fascination and increase the potential mystique of this sort of person. There is much here to fascinate the world and very little that could be called negative. Truly understanding Aquarius with Pisces Rising may prove impossible, however, and most people allied to the combination for any length of time probably won't try.

Chapter 25

Rising Signs for Pisces

Pisces with Aries Rising

This is a combination of zodiac signs that can seem puzzling to the outsider and even to the individual who possesses it. Aries and Pisces don't really have very much in common and it is difficult to envisage someone who is both progressive and sensitive. For much of the time, Pisces, the Sun Sign here, predominates, creating a caring, friendly and affable disposition. Only occasionally will the world become aware of a latent desire to push forward aggressively.

Pisces with Aries Rising requires stability but may be restless and inclined to travel a good deal. On the level of work, significant success can be expected. Friendships are formed early in life and maintained. Once these individuals set their hearts upon a particular course, little or nothing will hold them back.

Pisces with Taurus Rising

We are hardly likely to find either the noisiest or most gregarious person in this combination. On the contrary, although friendly and approachable, Pisces with Taurus Rising is quiet, contemplative and serene. Taurus brings a capable streak and the nature is altogether committed to peace, harmony and the pursuit of artistic interests. However, when necessary, this individual may display a stubborn streak and with it a refusal to do anything against their will.

Pisces with Taurus Rising is concerned about the world and anxious to help whenever possible. The usual Piscean approach to relationships is quite obvious here but the level of constancy and loyalty is greatly increased. These individuals take personal attachments particularly seriously and tend to make them long-lasting. Look out for a wistful quality and a serenity of nature that is extremely attractive to others. Pisces with Taurus Rising also has a strong desire to form relationships that bring a degree of protection and security. Younger family members are deemed especially important to this zodiac sign combination and the level of commitment to the world at large is very strong.

Pisces with Gemini Rising

Pisces and Gemini are both 'dual' signs – one showing two fish and the other a pair of twins – and, as a combination, they tend to work very well together. What really sets these individuals apart is their unpredictability. Always changeable, but ever affable and kind, Pisces with Gemini Rising seeks to achieve a high level of popularity and is particular committed to service. There is little about this nature that could be considered contentious, though it is given to taking strange courses of action and possesses qualities that may be puzzling and occasionally truly astonishing. Concentration may be a problem for this type.

In terms of relationships, this person has many friends and also desires to create a settled and even conservative home life. However, this potential is often subverted by the very restlessness that Gemini brings to the personality. Generally kind and sympathetic, Pisces with Gemini Rising has a great influence on almost anyone it encounters.

Pisces with Cancer Rising

This is the first of the double Water-sign combinations with the sign of Pisces. When allied to Cancer, Pisces shows a much stronger than usual desire to nurture and protect, particularly at a family level. The same is broadly true with friendships and this is someone who shows tremendous compassion for the underdog, as well as a desire to make the world a better place for everyone. Personal success may be limited by an in-built desire for security that may make them cling to things, and even people on occasions.

Nobody would doubt this person's desire to do the right thing, under almost all circumstances. Though not loud or contentious, Pisces with Cancer Rising can fight tenaciously when required, even if it tends not to do so for its own sake.

Pisces with Leo Rising

Leo is a very good zodiac Rising Sign for any Pisces because it strengthens the potential, invigorates the nature and ensures a higher degree of material success than might otherwise be the case. Although there is little about this individual that would be considered contentious or aggressive, the Piscean nature, which so often tends to prefer to maintain an acceptable status quo, in this combination is given a much more progressive feel and a desire to move forward, bringing good material gains and an ability to occupy positions of authority.

Like all Pisceans, this example is quite happy to offer support and encouragement to those who are struggling. Often to be found working in the caring professions, Pisces with Leo Rising does have an ability to reach the top in its chosen career and is generally happier at work than most people born under the sign of the Fishes. There is a strong commitment to love and marriage, together with a desire for a settled life.

Pisces with Virgo Rising

In many respects this might appear to be one of the quietest Piscean combinations, yet Virgo does bestow the ability to get its message across when necessary. Practical skills are useful to Piscean types and Virgo in the mix tends to bring them to the fore. This is certainly not someone who would be happy to sit around and watch the rest of the world doing things but rather a person who is willing and able to get stuck in to almost any task.

The attitude towards relationships of a personal nature is steady and very secure. Pisces with Virgo Rising may often commit to marriage early in life and will then stick to the relationship through thick and thin. A tiny hint of dissatisfaction with convention is present here, though perhaps without the strength of mind to replace it with something new. The nervous system isn't strong in this mix and frequent periods of rest are likely and essential.

Pisces with Libra Rising

Pisces allied with Libra leads to a generally happy nature and one that is extremely committed to making the world a fairer place for everyone concerned. Never argumentative and always the diplomat, this sort of individual is unlikely ever to become involved in any sort of contentious issue. Pisces with Libra Rising does, nevertheless, have ways and means of getting its message across and is deeply concerned with the way it appears to the world at large.

One of the most likeable types of already affable Pisces, this individual attracts friends easily and tends to keep them. People naturally turn to Pisces with Libra Rising for advice and can expect a balanced view of any situation, together with practical assistance of a considered and sensible sort. This character has no difficulty in committing to love, marriage and family responsibilities.

Pisces with Scorpio Rising

These individuals are often at odds with themselves, though rarely in a way that will make waves for others. They are often dissatisfied and are constantly making small changes to their lives. Frequent career moves are common with this combination, as is the tendency to move home fairly often. A more settled attitude does develop with the passing of time and this may coincide with a stronger feeling of both personal and financial security.

Pisces with Scorpio Rising loves with a genuine passion and is able to demonstrate its deep affection in very practical ways. Often given to jealousy, it nevertheless forgives more easily than Scorpio would and almost always seeks compromises. There is some need for travel within this mix and the possibility of life far away from home. Artistic inclinations are paramount and should be catered for at every level. Hardship in later life is almost unheard-of with this combination.

Pisces with Sagittarius Rising

This is a most unusual character but one who is popular, outgoing, extremely socially inclined and very balanced in attitude. The zodiac signs of Pisces and Sagittarius don't really have much in common, though in terms of this combination their differences actually allow for better prospects than either zodiac sign would normally expect. The somewhat restricted attitude of Pisces is enlivened by Sagittarius, whilst the sign of the Fishes deepens the usually shallow nature of the Archer. All in all, the result is balance, allied to both sociability and compassion.

In Pisces with Sagittarius Rising we should not expect to find an over-complicated nature. On the contrary, this is probably the most laid-back Piscean of them all. Nevertheless commitments, especially personal ones, are taken very seriously and when this zodiac combination loves, it does so completely and with great loyalty.

Pisces with Capricorn Rising

All Pisceans want to help; that's the hallmark of this zodiac sign and it doesn't change when Capricorn is in the mix. In fact, the kind of assistance that can be offered here is of a very practical and enduring sort. Although generally friendly, Pisces with Capricorn Rising is also quite quiet and is not inclined to push itself forward, especially in social situations. It has the capacity to be quite successful in a material sense and maintains an ability to persist, even when others have fallen by the wayside.

Pisces with Capricorn Rising has much to offer the world and is particularly keen on establishing a settled personal and family life as soon as possible. Not particularly inclined to travel, this sign combination will often stay for its whole life close to where it was born. Sometimes accused of lacking imagination, though always caring and desirous of the well-being of others, this is a character that demonstrates great stability.

Pisces with Aquarius Rising

Pisces with Aquarius Rising is certainly not likely to be lacking in popularity. This person always has something interesting to say, is very rarely conventional and is given to shocking others, almost as a matter of course. All the same, there is nothing especially contentious about this nature, which remains compassionate, committed and, at the end of the day, steadfast. On the way, there is some eccentricity and much originality, often displayed in terms of domestic surroundings or personal style.

Pisces with Aquarius Rising is fond of travel and possesses great insight into the way others think. Its ability to get on well with people on a close personal level is partly born out of this natural intuition, which it can also use to achieve material success. A good and entertaining friend, this is someone who enjoys great popularity.

Pisces with Pisces Rising

Double Pisces is magnetic, charming, quiet and caring. It longs to find protection for its relationships and often allies itself with far stronger people. Ready to serve and always willing to see an alternative point of view, double Pisces is the peacemaker and cannot live in a world of argument or aggression. It has a completely natural sense of order and beauty, but sometimes has to settle for confusion, which it may unintentionally create.

Personal attachments are very important to this individual, who often settles on the first potential romantic relationship that comes along. There is nothing especially impulsive in this tendency – it is simply born out of a need to belong. However, there can be problems in love and marriage for double Pisces, though a strong inclination for ultimate happiness usually secures contentment eventually. The most significant characteristic is the help this sort of person can offer to the world.

Index